Life Stories of
SIKH GURUS

B. Chattar Singh Jiwan Singh

AMRITSAR, (Pb.) INDIA

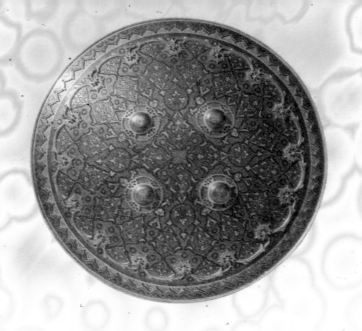

Life Stories of
SIKH GURUS

Second Edition March 2006
ISBN : 81-7601-628-4
Price : 200-00/-

Publisher :
B. Chattar Singh Jiwan singh
Bazar Mai Sewan, Amritsar. (Pb.) INDIA
Phone : +91-183-2542346, 2557973, 2547974
Fax : 2557973
E mail : csjs@vsnl.com, csjsexports@vsnl.com
Visit us at : www.csjs.com

Printed in INDIA at Jiwan Printers, 312, East Mohan Nagar, Amritsar.
Phone : +91-183-2705003, 5095774

CONTENTS

ੴ

ਸਤਿ ਨਾਮੁ ਕਰਤਾ ਪੁਰਖੁ ਨਿਰਭਉ

ਨਿਰਵੈਰੁ ਅਕਾਲ

ਮੂਰਤਿ ਅਜੂਨੀ ਸੈਭੰ

ਗੁਰ ਪ੍ਰਸਾਦਿ

SRI GURU NANAK DEV JI

The benefactor God listened to the cries of human beings and sent Guru Nanak to this world. With the emergence of the true Guru, the mist cleared and the light scattered all around. As if at the rise of the sun, the stars disappear and the darkness dispells. Wherever the Guru put his feet a religious place was established.

Guru Nanak was born on (Kattak full moon night) October 20, 1469 A.D. at Talwandi Raae Bhoe in District Shekhupura, forty miles to the south-west of Lahore.

The village Talwandi later on came to be known as Nankaana Sahib, now in Pakistan. The name of his father was Mehta Kalyan Dass which was affectionately abridged by the people as Mehta Kaalu.

The name of his mother was Tripta Devi and his sister Nanaki was five

years his senior.

In our country the birth of a male child is considered to be very fortunate. When the midwife came out and announced that a male child was born, Mehta Kaalu felt very happy. The midwife Daultan also told him that at the time of the birth of the child, a beam of light flashed across the room and strange and sweet voices were heard as welcoming the child. The child was not an ordinary child, instead of weeping, he smiled.

On seeing the child Pandit felt an everlasting peace and tranquilness. He paid homage to the child with folded hands.

While making the horoscope Pandit Hardyal said, "He would be a great

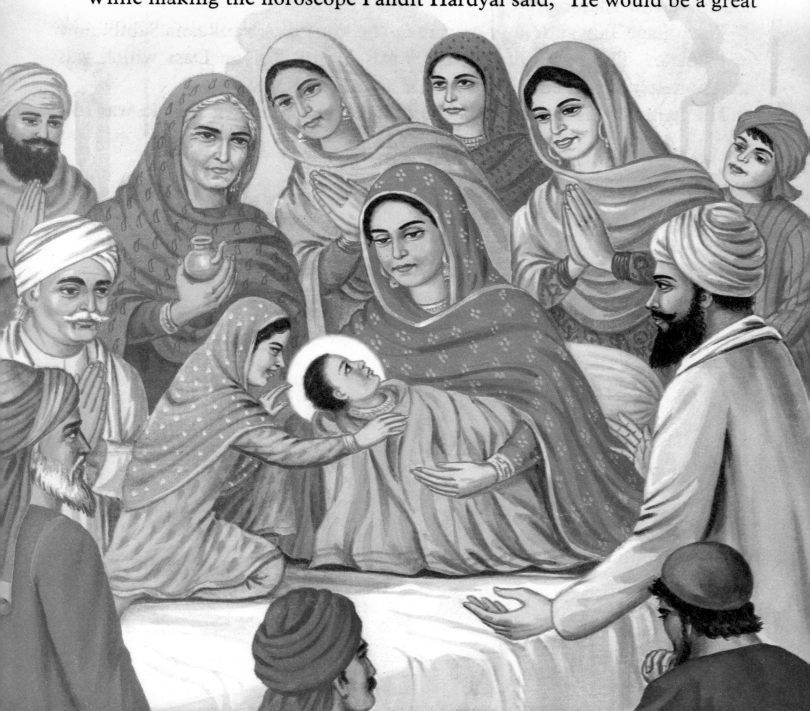

Divine King. Both Hindus and Muslims will reverence him. He will be King of the kings. He will believe and worship only One Formless, Omnipotent and Graceful God. He will consider every creature as the creation of the God. He will lead a new unique sect which will be eternal."

Guru Nanak was a very fascinating child. He was not an ordinary child. Children of his age liked him very much and everyone wanted to play with him. But his games and toys were different from other children. In his early age he used to talk about the Supreme Soul and the path of religion and good deeds. He loved those people very much who were contemplating on the Name of God. He had a great regard for saints and holy persons. He

served those people gladly.

When the Guru was of six years old then his father Mehta Kaalu got him admitted in the village school, whose incharge was Pandit Gopal Dass. Pandit was a scholar of Punjabi, Hindi and Sanskrit. The Guru showed keen interest in his studies and quickly learnt everything that the Pandit could teach him. The Pandit was wonder struck to see the supernatural brain of his student.

Guru Nanak's genius for poetry was acknowledged by Pandit Gopal Dass.

When the Guru became proficient in Punjabi, Hindi and Sanskrit then he was got admitted in the Maktab (Persian and Arabic School) maintained by Maulvi Qutab-ud-Din. In those days the official language of the government was Persian.

So it was very important for the public to learn Persian in order to get government jobs. Mehta Kaalu also desired to make his son an official of the Pathan government.

When Nanak entered the ninth year it was decided to celebrate the Janeoo sacrament. A day was fixed to perform the ceremony and messages were sent to all relatives and friends. After doing all necessary rites, Pandit leaned forward to place the cord across the shoulder of Nanak. As the ceremony was going to be completed so all the relatives and friends were making themselves ready to congratulate Mehta Kaalu. But all were astonished when they saw Nanak pushing back the thread towards Pandit. He denied to wear the thread.

One day Mehta Kaalu thought that Nanak should be sent to graze the cattle. He had many cows and buffaloes and had employed a servant to take the cattle out for grazing but his work was not satisfactory. So he asked Nanak to do that job. Nanak was very fond of roaming in the forests and mountains. So he readily accepted the proposal. He used to take buffaloes to green meadows, dense forests and vast pastures. But while grazing the cattle, he would fix his mind on one God.

One day when it was very hot summer noon the Guru drove the cattle towards one shady tree. The buffaloes felt relieved standing under that tree and the Guru also put his long towel on the ground and sat down. After sometime Nanak lay down and fell asleep. With the passing of the time the shade of the tree shifted and hot rays of sun began to fall on his naked face. Suddenly a big cobra came and spread out its large hood over the face of the sleeping Nanak.

By chance ruler of the village named Raae Bulaar was returning home with his servants, after assessing the ripened crops. When they came near that shady tree, Raae Bulaar was alarmed to see the Guru lying fast asleep unaware of a big cobra beside him. He at once ordered his servants to rush on that direction with sticks in their hands.

When the cobra saw some one coming towards him, it vanished into the near by shrubs. In the meantime Raae Bulaar

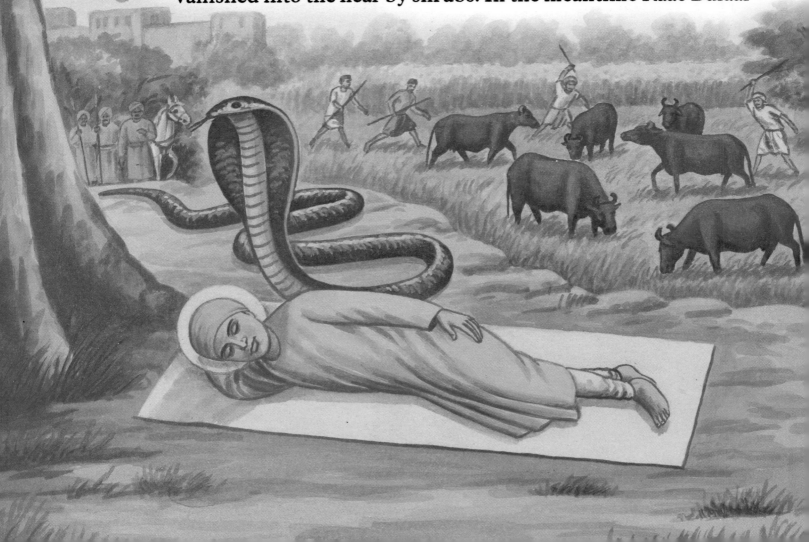

approached near Nanak and found him fast asleep. He was pleased to see Nanak alive. His servants told him that when they came near, the cobra folded its hood and ran away. They felt ashamed that they could not kill it. But Raae Bulaar said, "The cobra was not an ordinary snake, the God had sent him to protect Guru Nanak from the scorching heat of the sun. The cobra had not approached Nanak to kill him, but it had come there to provide him shade."

One day Mehta Kaalu gave him twenty silver rupees and asked him to invest the sum usefully. He also advised him to go to town Chooharkaana and purchase such goods which he could sell at a profit.

Guru Nanak took his friend Bhai Baala with him and set out for Chooharkaana. On their way to Chooharkaana there lay a jungle full of thick bushes. There in a grove they spotted a large party of bare-skinned Saadhus.

Nanak found that the saints had been hungry since many days. He made up his mind to feed those hungry men. Guru Nanak took Bhai Baala with him and they marched towards Chooharkaana. There they hired a cart and bought the ration and clothings for the hungry men. Then Guru Nanak and Bhai Baala served the prepared food to the hungry saints. Guru Nanak was very happy because it was the best-bargain he could strike with his money.

After sometime the Guru remained silent and did not wish to come out of his home. He was always meditating on the Name of God and became immersed in his own thoughts. He ate and drank very little and always remained lying on his bed. His parents were much grieved and they were thinking that some thing serious had happened to Nanak.

At last Mehta Kaalu brought Hardaas, the village physician. Hardaas held the wrist of Nanak with in his fingers and began to feel the pulse. The Guru looked keenly towards the face of the physician and smiled. Then the serious patient burst into laughter and said, "O physician! What are you seeing, I am quite healthy, the sickness which you are searching with your fingers is not of the body. You can not diagnose it. It is beyonds your knowledge."

Physician heard Guru's word very patiently. Then saying, "Nanak is hale and hearty," he left the house.

Jai Ram, the brother-in-law of Guru Nanak had a great regard in the court of Nawab Daulat Khan Lodhi. One day he introduced Nanak to

Nawab, who was very impressed to have a glimpse of such a charming personality. Whatever question he asked him, Guru replied with great confidence and competence. Nawab was struck by his answers and forthwith made him incharge of his stores. He fixed his salary and ration. Guru Nanak liked that service. But doing Nawab's service he had not forgotten to contemplate on the Name of God. Daily he arose early in the morning and walked to rivulet Bein. He bathed and then remained absorbed in reciting Name of the Almighty.

Guru Nanak was eighteen, when the marriage took place. His marriage was fixed on 24, Jeth 1544 B.K. Mehta Kaalu, Mata Tripta and their all relatives, friends reached Sultanpur Lodhi. Thus the wedding party was formed in Sultanpur Lodhi.

After marriage the Guru brought Mata Sulakhani to Sultanpur Lodhi. His parents returned to Talwandi after staying for sometime with their son.

In Sultanpur Lodhi were born both of Guru Nanak's sons. The elder son Sri Chand was born in 1494 A.D. and Lakhmi Chand in 1496 A.D.

When Guru Nanak was residing at Sultanpur Lodhi, he needed a musical instrument that could help him in singing his hymns. Many Dhaadis and folk singers were also attending his Satsang (holy assembly). One of these folk singer was Bhai Pharinda (Phera Rababi). He used to sing his folk songs with the help of a Rabab (a folk musical instrument). One day the Guru asked Bhai Pharinda to prepare a beautiful Rabab for him. Bhai Pharinda who belonged to village Bhairowal (Kapurthala) presented a Rabab to the Guru. When the Guru tuned it then a sweet, melodious resonance resounded. The Guru liked it very much.

When Mardaana attended the marriage of Guru then he asked the Guru for the marriage gift. The Guru handed over that Rabab to Mardaana as a gift. Bhai Mardaana deemed himself exalted by having such a pleasant

musical instrument. Then the Guru advised Mardaana to stay with him. Mardaana readily accepted and later he became a life long companion of the Guru.

Nanak used to go to Bein river to perform his ablutions. In early years he was going alone, but after that his disciples also followed him and after bathing they meditated on the Name of God. One day Nanak did not come out of the river after ablutions. His friends became worried and they tried their best to search. When they could not trace him, they at once informed Diwan Jai Ram and Bebe Nanaki. They all thought that he had been drowned in the river. Nanak was not an ordinary man. The people of city had a great regard and love for him. Such a news caused a gloom in the city. The people ran towards the river. Nawab Daulat Khan himself visited the site. His divers and fishermen threw nets into the river to search for the body.

On the third day the citizens were amazed to see him hale and hearty.

Nanak sat on the bank of Bein and remained silent. When the next day he spoke, he said, "There is only One God and there is no Hindu and there is no Musalman but all are equal."

One day Qazi said to Nawab that if Nanak considers Hindus and Muslims equal and had declared that there was no difference between these two religions then he should join us during the evening prayer. Nawab sent a messenger and requested the Guru to join them during the evening Namaz. Guru Nanak agreed and went to mosque. There he accompanied the Nawab and the Qazi. As the Qazi was conducting the service, the Guru did not kneel and remained standing. He saw towards Qazi and smiled. After the service was over the Qazi complained to Nawab.

The Guru said, "What prayer was I expected to join. I smiled because Qazi's prayer was not accepted by the God though obviously he was praying, because his heart was not in the words he was repeating. His mind was wandering in his house. Immediately before the prayer service, he had loosened his new born foal in his courtyard. There is a well in his courtyard. While he was performing Divine service his mind was filled with fear lest the foal should fall into the well." When Nawab asked Qazi

about it, the Qazi admitted that the Guru had spoken truth. But the Qazi said, "It is true my mind was wandering and I worried about the foal, but you should have joined the Nawab. The Guru smiled and said, "Nawab was also not here. While he was pretending to pray, his mind was wandering in Kabul and he was thinking of purchasing horses." The Nawab also admitted the statement of the Guru. The Nawab and Qazi were so much moved on hearing the true statements of the Guru that they prostrated at his feet.

Guru Nanak dressed himself in a strange garb and set out to redeem the world and human kind. He set out on his travels with his companion Mardaana.

They travelled towards north west and reached Saidpur. As they were wearing an uncommon costume, they had a great attraction for the people of Saidpur.

In their way they saw a carpenter sitting in the courtyard making wooden agricultural tools with chisel and saw. When the Guru reached near him he said, "Bhai Laalo! How are you." Bhai Laalo was startled on hearing his name from the lips of a strange man. He at once got up and joined his rugged hands in salutation. He welcomed the strange visitors and requested them to accompany him in to his house.

He offered them a cot and prayed them to take rest and feel at home.

This was Guru's first halt in the house of his first Sikh.

There lived a Hindu named Malik Bhaago. He was a steward of the local Muslim chief. He announced a grand feast and invited every caste-Hindu, all saints and faqirs.

Guru Nanak was also invited. Reaching there Guru Nanak said, "Mr. Malik ! Your food is not pure. I can not eat an impure food. Your blood soaked food does not agree with me so I do not like to take it." The Malik said, "It means the delicious dishes prepared by me are impure and are polluted with blood instead the crumbs of the Laalo's house are pure. How dare you say so, you should explain me how you made this bold statement?"

On hearing this Guru Nanak became serious. He said boldly that he would prove what he had said. He asked the Malik to bring the so called very delicious food from his kitchen. At the same time he asked for food to be brought from the house of Laalo. Then Guru Nanak took the Laalo's course bread in his right hand and Malik Bhaago's delicious sweet breads in his left

hand.

Guru pressed his both hands, milk dropped from course bread of Bhai Laalo and blood oozed from Malik Bhaago's delicacies.

The Guru's way of preaching was very dramatic. He always visited the holy places on the occasion of big fairs. Once Guru Nanak visited Kurukshetra. On that day a big fair was held due to Solar eclipse. A large number of people had gathered there. Many Brahmans and holy saints had come there to attend the fair. Some were bathing in the Sarswati and others were sitting on the bank of the river.

The Guru Nanak asked his Sikhs to bring a big pot and to fill that with some water. Then he asked them to light the fire and place the pot on it.

When the Pandits saw the fire they at once ran towards him. They asked the Guru to extinguish the fire. But the Guru paid no heed towards them. They cried very loudly and the Brahman chief said, "What are you cooking." The Guru replied that he was cooking meat. Hearing this they became very

furious and called that act of grave profanation. They accused him of sacrilege. But the Guru said calmly, "Your beliefs are false and the story of Raahu and Kettu is imaginary. Nothing would happen.

Preaching his holy message the Guru reached Haridwar, when the Guru reached there a big fair was being held there. Thousands of people had gathered there to take bath in the holy river. Guru Nanak stood with the pilgrims on the Khushwant Ghaat, where the water of river was considered to be the holiest. The pilgrims dipped themselves in the river to perform their ablutions. They prayed and tossed water in palmsful towards the rising sun. It was their belief that by doing so, they were offering water to their forefathers.

The Guru began to throw the water to the west. The Brahmans and other people were surprised to see this. They wondered that nobody had ever done such an act before. Many Brahmans and pilgrims gathered around him.

They asked, "Why are you offering water towards the west?" The Guru said, "I am watering my fields. There is my farm in Punjab which needs watering." The pilgrims felt amused and said, "How far are your fields from

here?" The Guru replied that those were about two hundred Kos away. Then the Guru asked, "How far are your forefathers from here?" They said, "Our ancestors are in the next world. The distance is beyond our imagination."

When the Guru and Bhai Mardaana reached Patna the Guru gave Mardaana a piece of precious jewel and asked him to go into the city to meet Saalis Raae, jeweller. Mardaana at once reached the shop of Saalis Raae and said, "My master has sent me to sell this jewel, please check it and pay me the reasonable price." Saalis Raae took the jewel and when he scanned it, he was wonder struck. He handled the stone very carefully and kept on seeing towards it very curiously. Then he gave one hundred rupees to Mardaana and also returned the jewel and said, "This is a very costly jewel, I cannot pay its price. But I am giving you hundred rupees as the fee of having a glimpse of such a costly jewel." Mardaana was also surprised to hear this. He met the Guru and narrated him the jewel's episode. The Guru declined to take the money and asked Bhai Mardaana to return the money back to the jeweller. Mardaana went back and handed back the money to the jeweller. He said, "My master does not want money. He is a Saint and he is devoid of wordly attractions." Saalis Raae became very anxious to see his master.

Mardaana led him and they reached the place where the Guru was sitting. He bowed before the Guru and placed their presents and gifts in front of him. The Guru smiled and asked him to sit. The Guru explained them about the path of Sikhism and he became true follower of the Guru.

The Guru arrived in Kamroop the land of magic and witchcraft. The ruler of the city was a very beautiful queen named Noor Shah.

One day Mardaana requested the Guru to allow him to see the beauty of that fascinating city. The Guru said, "Do go if you want, but you should beware that this city is commanded by witches. They befool the newcomers." When he reached at the door of the Noor Shah's house, she enchanted him with her charming beauty and sweet words.

Soon Mardaana became unconscious and fell asleep. The Guru waited for sometime and then he set out in search of him. He entered the house of Noor Shah and asked her about Mardaana. The Guru tuned the 'Rabab' and began to sing his hymn.

When Bhai Mardaana heard the voice of his master, the spell of magic

vanished and he awoke up and coming outside bowed before the Guru. Noor Shah was astonished to see Mardaana all the better. Though she wanted to charm the Guru but she was herself enchanted. She threw her scarf round her neck in penitence and bowed before the Guru. She became a Sikh of the Guru. She freed her slaves and distributed her property within the poor. She became a preacher of Sikhism.

Guru Nanak reached the temple of Jagannath, Lord of the Earth. One day chief priest of the temple invited the Guru to join the evening service of lights in the temple. The Guru agreed to go with him.

In the evening the priests lighted the tiny lamps. They placed these lamps on a jewel studded salver. Then they put some flowers and incense on it and swung the salver from side to side in front of the idol of Lord Krishna. They also chanted some holy hymns and blew conches and rang the bells. But the Guru did not participate in the ceremony. The priests felt very angry and they complained the Guru about this. Then the Guru said, "Your this homage is too small for a God as high as the Lord of the Universe." Then he sang a hymn in praise of the Supreme Lord which is unrivalled in the whole gamut of world poetry. *"Gagan Mai Thaal Rav Chand Deepak Bane."*

When the Guru reached Sialkot, he took his seat under a Ber tree. There he learnt that the Peer Hamza Gauns had laid the town under a curse of destruction. The Guru tried to meet the Faqir, but every time Mardaana was sent back by his attendants. When the people of Sialkot came to know that Guru Nanak had been sitting under the shade of a Ber tree, they thronged to meet him. They requested the Guru to protect them from the fury of that Peer. Guru Nanak said to them, "Don't worry? The tomb of the room will automatically burst in the mid-day and the Chalihaa of the Faqir will remain incomplete." The people of the city felt some relief.

At noon they saw that the tomb of the room cracked and fell apart and the Peer rushed out of the room. He was so horrified that he forgot all about the Chalihaa. When his attendants told him about the Guru, he came to see him. The Guru advised him, "You must not blame the sins of one man upon all the inhabitants of the city. You are a holy man. It is the duty of the holy men to serve the people instead of destroying them."

Peer Hamza Gauns became a Sikh of the Guru.

From Sialkot the Guru and Bhai Mardaana travelled towards west. They reached Mithankot where a Peer, named as Mithe Shah lived. He was considered to be possessing many miraculous powers.

One day Peer met the Guru and said, "You are a Hindu Faqir, who is your god?" The Guru replied, "Mian Mithe Shah ! First sit down comfortably. I have come here to relinquish your doubts. I believe in One God, the Almighty. I do not worship a god made of stone. If the idol is god then all other stones must also be gods. Those who fall at the feet of the stone idol, their service is futile."

The Peer was astonished to hear such a clear cut reply of the Guru. Then to clarify his doubt he said, "But you must be believing in one prophet. Without prophet a man cannot attain unity with God." The Guru advised him, "God has always revealed Himself as eternal Light. Perfect vision is the vision of God's light and beauty. There is no need of god, or prophet to get enlightenment. These gods and prophets are all dependent upon God. Muslims seek the help of prophet and Hindus depend upon gods. Then what is the difference between these two religions. I do not believe in gods who live only in heaven. God is immense and omnipresent.

Next place where the Guru and Bhai Mardaana reached was the kingdom of Raja Shiv Nabh. When the Guru and Bhai Mardaana reached the city of Raja Shiv Nabh they took up their dwelling in one garden of Shiv Nabh. The news spread through out the city that a holy man from another country had arrived in the city. When the Raja heard this news, he was pleased that the Guru might have come. But before going to see him, he made certain tests. But when he was assured that the Guru himself had come, he felt very happy. He took his wives and children to pay homage to the great Guru. When he reached the garden, on seeing the divine Guru, he fell at his feet. Then he asked some questions and Guru Nanak satisfied him. The Guru granted him the knowledge of the mystery of existence.

Raja Shiv Nabh and his family became Guru's disciples. Raja established there a Temple where holy assembly was held and holy hymns were recited in praise of God.

Then the Guru and Bhai Mardaana reached Gorakh Mata, there they sat down under a withered tree. That tree became green and shady. It put on new

foliage. When the Yogis saw this strange phenomenon, they wondered. They came to talk with Guru. They said, "O youngman! Who is your Guru, from whom had you received teachings?" The Guru uttered a hymn and told them that his Guru was beyond description." The yogis were much impressed to hear the hymn of the Guru. The yogis bowed before the Guru in reverence. Later on Gorakh Mata came to be known as Nanak Mata.

From there the Guru and Bhai Mardaana travelled towards north and on their way they sat under the shade of a tree to take rest. There, when Mardaana complained of hunger, then the Guru pointing towards one branch of the Soapnut tree, asked him to eat the fruit. When Mardaana plucked some fruits of that branch he found those very sweet and eatable. When he tried to pluck the fruit of another branch he found that very bitter. That tree still exists and pilgrims from far and near come to see it throughout the year. These days a very beautiful Gurdwara has been constructed at that place. This Gurdwara is known as Reetha Sahib.

Then the Guru crossed many mountain ranges and ascended the Sumer Parbat. There he met Sidhas. The Sidhas were astonished to see two travellers coming from the earthly world. They atonce questioned the Guru, "O youngman listen ! What power is it that has brought you here?" The Guru replied, "I worship One God and I meditate on His Name. By His power I have reached here safe and sound." Then the Sidhas said, "What is the condition of the earthly people? How do it fare with them, are they living peacefully?" Then the Guru said, "Oh Naths! In which capacity can you ask about the earthly people, when you have hidden yourself in these high mountains. You are so coward that you do not even dare to go there to save those people. Do you know that darkness over spreads the world, the moon of earth is invisible. The earth is groaning under the weight of unjustness.

On hearing the Guru all Sidhas became dumb.

Arriving at Mecca, Guru Nanak felt tired. He had travelled a long and arduous journey to reach the holy city. He fell asleep. He slept with his feet towards Kaaba instead of his head. It was against the principles of Islam.

When at night a Qazi came there he saw him lying in that posture. He was enraged to see the Guru sleeping with feet pointing towards Kaaba, the house of God. He cried, "O man, do you not see? Why are you stretching your feet towards the House of God?" The Guru awoke and said, "O man of God, I am very tired, please turn my feet towards that direction where God is not." Then the Qazi dragged his feet round. But in whatever direction, he turned his feet, Kaaba also turned to that direction. Qazi was stunned. He said to himself, "Where God is not, His abode is in all four directions." He placed the Guru Nanak's feet on the ground and fell on them. He said, "Wonderful! Today I have seen a true faqir of God." When other pilgrims heard about this they gathered on the spot. They asked him many questions. They had discovered that Guru Nanak was a Hindu by birth. Therefore their main question was, "Who was the superior Hindu or Musalman?" The Guru answered, Without good deeds both are useless. Neither the Hindu nor the Musalman would be acceptable to the God." Then they travelled further across the Arabian desert and reached Baghdad

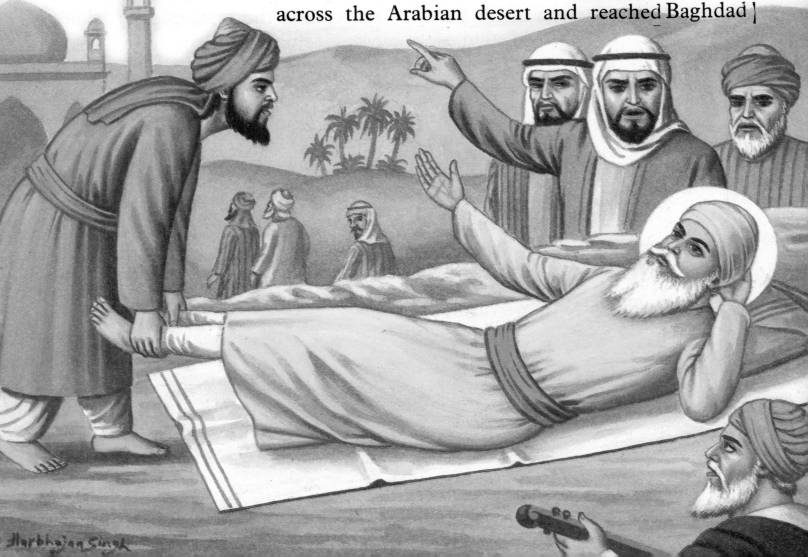

In the evening he uttered a call to prayer in the style of Muslims. He uttered the call in such a sweet and loud voice that people of Baghdad were enchanted to hear it. They flocked to see the Faqir. On hearing Peer Dastgir himself turned up and sat near him. His learned son and other followers were also with him. The Peer said, "Who are you and to which dynasty of Faqirs you belong?" The Guru answered, "My name is Nanak and I believe in One God. As God does not belong to any dynasty, religion and country, so being His humble servant, I do not belong to any dynasty, religion and country. There are millions of heaven and millions of underworlds. He is present everywhere."

Peer Dastgir was astonished to hear such a answer from Guru Nanak. But son of Peer said, "We believe in seven heavens and seven underworlds. How can you claim millions of heavens and underworlds."

Then the Guru placed his hand on the forehead of the son of the Peer and asked him to close his eyes. Then with in a few minutes Peer's son saw millions of heavens and underworlds. He told all about these worlds to his associates. All fell on|the feet of Guru.

Then he crossed the Indus and came to Hasan Abdal. It was a small village situated near the back of a hill. On the top of the hill there lived a Muslim Peer. He was known as Baba Wali Kandhaari.

On the top of the hill near the abode of Baba Wali Kandhaari there was a big tank full of water. Mardaana feeling thirsty went up the hill to request the Wali Baba. But Wali refused to give him water. Then the Guru asked Mardaana to lift a small stone from the hill side. As he lifted the stone, water rushed out with force and flowed in the shape of a drain. Bhai Mardaana and other villagers drank to their fill. As the water from the new spring started to flow, Wali Baba's reservoir began to ebb. Soon the tank dried up. When he saw his reservoir dried up he became very angry. He was so enraged that he rolled a huge rock towards the Guru in order to kill him. When the Guru saw a big stone rolling down he raised his hand with open palm. The rock stopped in its downward course. As it touched the hand of the Guru, his palm made an impress upon it. Baba Wali Kandhaari was stunned to see it. He came down and fell at the feet of the Guru. The stone with palm-mark is still preserved on the site. This place is known as Gurdwara Panja Sahib.

Then they reached Saidpur (now known as Eminabad), he met his old friend Bhai Laalo. Soon thereafter Babar invaded the city of Saidpur.

Guru Nanak and Bhai Mardaana were also taken prisoners. When they reached at the camp they were asked to grind corn. Guru Nanak was also given a handmill to grind the corn. But the handmill of Guru Nanak worked by itself. The poor prisoners were sad and helpless. Guru Nanak's heart could not bear that. He burst forth and sang a hymn. His song made the prisoners to forget all about the handmills. When soldiers heard the melodious voice of the Guru, they were filled with wonder. A few of them went to tell Babar about the incident. Babar atonce rushed to the camp. He himself heard the sweet song of Guru Nanak. When the Guru stopped singing, Babar asked him to explain the meaning of the hymn. Guru Nanak explained him the meaning in Persian. He said, "I was singing about your cruelty and the plight of the victims. Those innocent people have done no harm to you. But you have killed and looted them mercilessly." Babar was impressed by Guru Nanak's courage. He released all the prisoners.

From Saidpur Guru Nanak and Bhai Mardaana reached Kartarpur.

After staying for one year at Kartarpur, Guru Nanak made another brief journey. There was a place named Achal near Batala. Achal was the centre of yogis. Guru Nanak had exposed the false tricks of yogis during the journeys but still they had some influence in Achal. They were against family life. They considered themselves holy religious leaders. Guru Nanak selected a place near the yogis. They sat under the shade of a jujube tree. He asked Mardaana to play on the rabab and the Guru started singing his divine hymns. When the people heard the voice of the Guru, they rushed to see him.

The people who were bowing and presenting gifts to the yogis, left that place and came to listen the Guru. The yogis were enraged. Their head yogi Bhangar Nath with some other yogis came to see Guru Nanak. He said, "Why have you rejected the religious garb and taken again worldly clothes." The Guru replied, "You have abandoned your family life and turned an anchorite, but still you beg at the doors of house holders. Your life depends upon their alms. It means family life is the finest form of life."

Reaching Multan, the Guru selected a place of their abode outside the city. There they were singing hymns in praise of God. When the people of

Multan heard about the arrival of the Guru, they flocked to pay homage to him. The fair which was being celebrated inside the city became manless. Peer, Faqirs were grieved to see this. One of them said, "Until or unless, the Guru does not leave Multan, we will be ruined. All our disciples and devotees are attending the Darbar of Guru Nanak. We should try to force Guru to leave Multan." Another said, "But it is not possible to force the Guru to leave the city. He has more followers than us. All those followers will go against us and instead of ousting the Guru, they will turn us out." So they thought a plan. They took a bowl brimful of milk and presented it to the Guru. The Guru asked the Peers to sit near him. He accepted the bowl very happily. The Guru atonce understood the hidden meaning of the presentation of the bowl brimful of milk. It indicated thereby that Multan was already full of holy men. There was no scope for another holy man to stay there. Guru Nanak put a Jasmine flower on the milk. The bowl did not overflow while the flower floated on it. In this way Guru Nanak spoke to the Peer of Multan in his own idiom. He told them without speaking that there was still room for a man like Nanak in their city. The Peers atonce

understood the meaning of the idiom pointed out by the Guru.

The Guru made Kartarpur as the centre of his teachings. He wrote his major poetic compositions there. During his vast travels the Guru had made many disciples. When they heard that the Guru had permanently settled at Kartarpur they started to reach there. The Guru established there a custom of singing in chorus the hymns in the morning as well as in the evening. Mardaana's son Shahzada was providing the music.

Most important institution was the 'Langar' or community meal. It was a symbol of brotherhood, equality and modesty. When Guru Ji merged his light into the light of God. Hindu and Muslim disciples quarrelled over the performance of last rites. But when they looked beneath the white shroud, they found there only beautiful white flowers. In his last message he also preached the brotherhood of mankind. The common food was eaten by people of all castes sitting in rows together. The Guru along with other followers tilled the farm, watered the fields and reaped the crops. Then Guru Nanak made up his mind to install Bhai Lehna as Guru. He addressed Lehna as Angad (part of his body).

SRI GURU ANGAD DEV JI

Bhai Lehna Ji who later on came to be known as Sri Guru Angad Dev Ji, was born on March 31, 1504 A.D. at Matte Di Saraan, district Mukatsar. His father Pheru Mal was well educated. He was working as an accountant of a Muslim ruler. The people of the village felt very happy when they heard news of the birth of Bhai Lehna. They came in the house of Bhai Pheru Mal to congratulate him.

In order to celebrate the birth of Bhai Lehna, the devotees came in large number. They sang songs in praise of Durga Maata. On seeing the beautiful child all were thanking the goddess.

When Bhai Lehna was sixteen years old Bhai Pheru Mal decided to get his son married. Bhai Lehna was married in village Khadoor near Tarn Taran in Amritsar district.

Harbhajan Singh

One day Bhai Jodha of his village was taking bath in the tank and was singing the sacred hymns. Bhai Lehna listened the hymns for a while, which caused strange effect on his mind. At that time Bhai Jodha was reciting the Pauri number twenty one of Aasa Di Vaar.

Bhai Lehna had never heard such sacred hymns in praise of God. He used only to listen and sing songs in praise of goddess.

He then said to Bhai Jodha "My friend! From where have you learnt these devotional songs? I also want to learn these songs." Bhai Jodha replied, "O great man ! These devotional songs have been composed by Guru Nanak." Then he told him about the life of Guru Nanak. He also told him that Guru Nanak speaks the word of God as it comes to him from God himself. "Who recites or listens these hymns, gets a glimpse of the true God and crosses peacefully this worldly ocean."

Next day Bhai Lehna took his horse and drove towards Kartarpur. When he reached near the village he saw a well built, healthy and tall old man. He drove near the old man and asked about the village and Guru Nanak's abode. That old man was Guru Nanak himself. Instead of pointing towards the residence of Guru Nanak, he asked him politely to follow him. Guru Nanak

guided him and Bhai Lehna, dismounting the horse, followed him. When they reached the Darbar of the Guru, pointing towards a peg, Guru Nanak asked him to tie his horse. Guru Nanak himself entered his room. He sat on his seat where he generally used to meet his devotees. Bhai Lehna asked from a Sikh about the whereabouts of Guru Nanak. The Sikh told him about the room of the Guru. But when Bhai Lehna entered the room he was astonished to see that the same old man who had led him the way, was Guru Nanak himself. Bhai Lehna was filled with shame and remorse.

Guru Nanak made Guru Angad Dev as his successor and advised him to go to his native village. The Guru Angad Dev Ji shifted to his village but was staying secretly in the house of Mai Virai. But the Sikhs felt worried as they could not find the whereabouts of the Guru.

But Bhai Buddha Ji was confident that the Guru must be in the house of Mai Virai. So he took five Sikhs and Rababi Balwand with him and reached the house of Mai Virai. Then he asked Bhai Balwand to tune his rebeck and to recite a hymn of Guru Nanak. Bhai Balwand recited a hymn of Guru Nanak in a very sweet and loud voice. When Guru Angad Dev heard the

voice of Bhai Balwand reciting a holy hymn of Guru Nanak he came outside and stood in the gate. He saw towards Baba Buddha and other Sikhs. He smiled and very happily said, "You have found the way how to locate the Guru." The recitation of the hymn of the Guru Nanak has such a power that no man on earth could resist it. Then at the request of Baba Buddha he agreed to go with them in order to see the Sikhs.

At the new place Khadur Sahib, on one side the Guru was showering the spiritual teachings to the people, and on the other side Mata Kheevi Ji wife of Guru Angad Dev Ji was supplying rich food to the Sikhs. She was made incharge of the langar and her duty was to supply food to all, irrespective of caste or creed.

Mata Ji used to get up early in the morning and after performing religious rites she attended the kitchen. Though there were other sewadars also to prepare and serve the food, but Mata Kheevi Ji himself prepared the vegetables and other dishes. She was keeping a watch in order to make it certain that all had been served according to their requirements. Bhai

Balwand Rababi writes, "Rice prepared in ghee were served to all."

Himayun once decided to proceed towards Khadur to meet Guru Angad Dev. When Himayun reached Khadur he was astonished to see the grandeur of the great Guru. At that time the Guru was delivering his divine sermons and his followers were listening him very carefully. When the Emperor tried to enter the Diwan Hall the sewaks stopped him. He felt offended and in fit of rage entered into the Diwan Hall forcefully and stood before the Guru. Instead of bowing before the Guru, he put his hand on the hilt of his

sword and drew it out in order to attack the Guru. Then the Guru with a smiling face looked at Himayun. Guru said, "Where was your sword at that time when you faced Sher Shah Suri? You did not dare to draw this sword out of your scabbard there. If you are so brave you should have cut off the head of Sher Shah with this sword.

The life history of Guru Nanak Dev was a great inheritance of Sikhs. So the Guru thought to write the complete life story of Guru Nanak Dev Ji.

At Sultanpur Lodhi there lived a Bhai Paira Mokha. He was an old Sikh of Guru Nanak. He was well versed in writing Gurmukhi neatly. So Guru Angad Dev Ji called Bhai Paira Mokha. Bhai Baala and Baba Buddha Ji in

order to write the Janam Saakhi. Every Saakhi was first discussed in detail with Bhai Baala, Baba Buddha Ji and Bhai Paira Mokha and then it was dictated to Paira Mokha. The whole Janam Saakhi was completed with in a year. Then Guru Ji prepared more copies of that manuscript.

In those days at Khadur Sahib lived a Jogi Tapa named as Shiv Nath. He was a great cheat and was befooling the common and simple people of the village. Once it so happened that there was no rains throughout the year. The crops withered away and cattle began to die due to hunger.

Worried farmers at last went to the Jogi Tapa. They asked him to perform Jantar Mantar to bring rain. Tapa said, "It does not rain due to presence of

Guru, oust him from the village and I will bring rain."

In the meantime a Sikh informed the Guru about the planning of the Jogi Tapa. The Guru left the village and went to another village. As Guru Angad Dev left the village, farmers asked Tapa to recite the Mantars. Tapa tried hard but his Mantars could not produce any result. Then farmers began to accuse him. They called him a deceit and repented about their false belief on Tapa.

Then Baba Amar Dass met the farmers and said, "There is only one method of getting the rain. You should take the Tapa in the fields. In which field he would stand, showers of rain would come." When the farmers took Tapa in one field they were astonished to see clouds in the sky and heavy rain came. They felt very pleased. Then every farmer became eager to take Tapa in his field. So the farmers dragged him from one field to another. They dragged Tapa with such a force that Tapa lost his life in this process. Tapa got the punishment for his evil deeds.

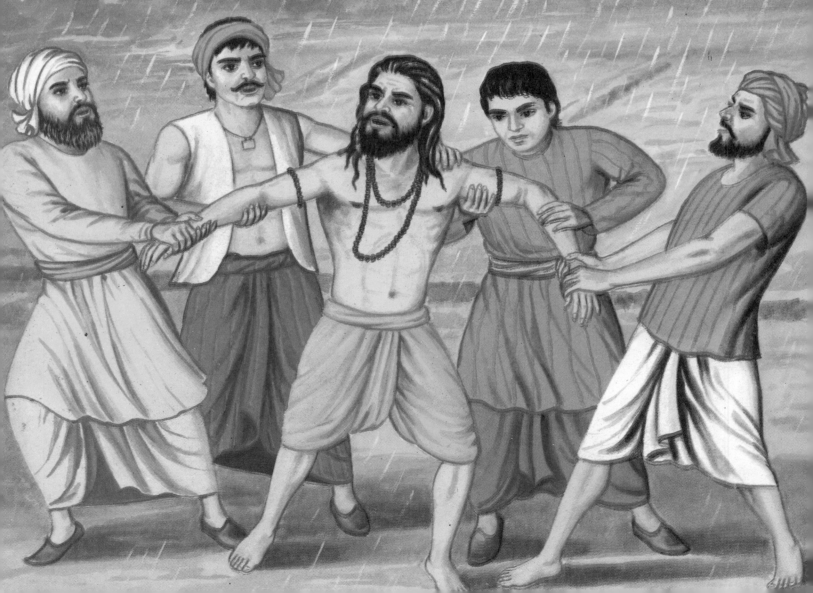

SRI GURU AMAR DASS JI

Guru Amar Dass was born on 5th May, 1479 A.D., at village Basarke in Amritsar. The name of his father was Baba Tej Bhan and mother's name was Mata Lakhmi.

One day early in the morning, Sri Amar Dass heard some hymns being sung in a sweet voice. That sweet voice was of Bibi Amaro. She was daughter of Guru Angad Dev Ji and was married to Bhai Jassu the nephew of Guru Amar Dass.

(Guru) Amar Dass was so enchanted that he instantly decided to meet Guru Angad Dev. He asked Bibi Amaro to accompany him in order to have glimpse of his father. Next day, they reached Khadur Sahib and (Guru) Amar Dass bowed before Guru Angad Dev with great reverence. He stayed there for few days and heard the recitation of the holy hymns. He was so impressed by the atmosphere of that place that he determined to stay there forever.

At last his service was acknowledged in the house of the Guru. Guru Angad Dev made up his mind to handover Guruship to (Guru) Amar Dass.

After constructing buildings in the land of Goinda, (Guru) Amar Dass also constructed inns and houses for the residence of Sikhs on that land which Goinda had offered to Guru Angad Dev. They also built shops and bazars for the outsiders and presented free to the needy persons.

So with in few months at the barren land of Goinda a beautiful city was

raised. On the name of Goinda the city was named as Goindwal.

When Guru Angad Dev Ji found that city had become fit for residence, he asked (Guru) Amar Dass to bring his family at Goindwal. (Guru) Amar Dass went to his village Basarke and asked his family to shift to Goindwal. They agreed and even his younger brothers and their families also shifted to Goindwal. But while staying at Goindwal (Guru) Amar Dass did not abandon his services towards Guru Angad Dev Ji.

Guru Amar Dass was installed as Guru on 29th March, 1552 A.D. He also shifted his headquarters from Khadur to Goindwal.

One day the Guru sent for his nephew Sawan Mal and handing to him a handkerchief, advised him to go to Raja Hari Chand of Haripur to make arrangements for the wooden building material. Bhai Sawan Mal reached Haripur and met Raja Hari Chand. He told him that he was disciple of Guru Amar Dass, who was third Guru Nanak. He informed them that his mission to come to state of Haripur was to supply wooden building material to Goindwal. Raja Hari Chand was very pleased to hear it. He said, "My friend! State of Haripur has such trees in abundance. I would be very lucky to supply

such wooden material to Goindwal.

Once Raja Hari Chand took his all queens and maids and set out for Goindwal. When they reached Goindwal, the Sikhs advised them that queens should wear simple dresses and no one should veil her face. When Raja and queens went inside to pay homage to the Guru, one queen veiled her face. When the Guru saw that one queen was concealing her face he said, "Who is this insane, who does not know the discipline of the house of the Guru and has come covering her face. If she was reluctant to see me, why has she come here?" When that queen heard those words of the Guru, she lost her senses and became insane. She atonce returned back and ran away towards the forests. The servants of Raja and Sikhs searched her for many days but they failed to find her anywhere.

One Sikh named Sachansach was a great devotee of the Guru. One day when he was going to forest to cut the trees, somebody caught him from behind with such a force that it became for him very difficult to get himself relieved from that strong grip. His axe fell down and the rope entangled his legs. When he unfettered himself with great force then he saw a mad girl standing before him. She was laughing like mad persons. When he advanced towards her she ran away and vanished in the forest.

So he got up early in the morning and met the Guru. He requested him to give him one wooden shoe so he might cure the insanity of the queen. The Guru smiled and gave one wooden shoe to Sachansach. Taking that wooden shoe with him he entered forest and began to search the queen. At one place by chance he saw the queen. But when the queen saw her, she ran away. He followed him and touched her with that wooden shoe. He saw another miracle. The queen stopped and feeling ashamed began to see towards her torn clothes. Bhai Sachansach gave her his turban and she worn the turban around her. Then Sachansach asked her to follow him. She came with him and he took her in front of the Guru. The Guru asked lady devotees to take her with them for bath. He also gave them nice clothes for her. When she came back after taking bath and wearing new clothes, she looked very beautiful. The Guru married her to Sachansach. The Guru gave them the second wooden shoe so that they might understand the secret of married life.

The Guru Amar Dass was so much loved by his devotees that they were daily going to Goindwal for an audience. But the younger son of Guru Angad Dev could not tolerate it.

In a fit of rage Daatu kicked the Guru in the back, making him fall of the throne and himself occupied his seat. Instead of getting annoyed the Guru held Daatu's foot and caressing it said, "I fear your foot is not hurt by hitting my old bones which have become stiff due to long service."

Next day, Guru Amar Dass took his mare and left Goindwal and went to his ancestral village Basarke and shut himself in a small room. He wrote a notice on the door saying, "He who tries to open this door is no Sikh of mine, nor I am his Guru."

Baba Buddha Guided the Sikhs and reached the place where Guru was hiding himself. On reading the words written on the door, they dug a big opening in the backside of the room. Baba Buddha Ji and companions entered into the room one by one. They found that the Guru was sitting in trance, contemplating on the Name of God.

Baba Budha Ji and other devotees requested the Guru to return back to Goindwal. The Guru Ji agreed to go with them. He mounted the mare and reached Goindwal.

The construction work for digging the step-well started in 1559 A.D. The

Sikhs worked hard and the Baoli was dug within few days. All steps were constructed and when Baoli was dug deep enough to strike water, they found that there was a rock which checked their further progress. All the workers came out of the well and requested the Guru for advice. After visiting the place himself the Guru said, "There is big rock under the base of the well. Until this rock is not blasted the water would not gush up. So now our first task is to blast this big slab. But I fear while blasting, the water would gush up with such a great force that it will rise up within moments. The man who does so would be overpowered by the gushing water and it is also possible he might be drowned."

When the devotees heard these words of the Guru they looked at one another. Who could take such a risk? But a brave son of Vairowal Sri Manak Chand atonce volunteered himself to go down the step-well to break the slab. The Guru handed over Sri Manak Chand a big hammer and blessed him that he would be successful in his mission. Sri Manak Chand took the hammer and went down the 'Baoli'. He struck the slab with such a great force that the

rock cracked and water gushed up with such a force that Sri Manak Chand was overpowered and drowned. But by Guru's grace soon he appeared out of the water and using the steps came out of the well. It is said that Guru declared that who-so-ever recites Japji once at every step would be free from the cycle of eighty-four-lakh births and deaths.

Once when Akbar was on his way back to Delhi, he visited Goindwal. As it was the ordain of the Guru, King Akbar with his ministers took meals in the common kitchen like other visitors. Akbar was very happy to sit with the lowest of the low and partaking of food with them. After taking the meals, Akbar met Guru Amar Dass and paid him a homage with great reverence. Then he sat near the Guru and had an audience with him. The Guru informed him about the aims of the Sikhism. Akbar was highly impressed to hear the sermons of the Guru.

SRI GURU RAM DASS JI

Guru Ram Dass was born on 25th September, 1534 A.D. in Chuna Mandi, Lahore. He was the son of Hari Dass Sodhi Khatri and Anupi Devi, known as Daya Kaur. He was named as Ram Dass but as he was the first child he was popularly known as Jetha. He had one younger brother Hardial and one younger sister Ram Dassi. He was fair of complexion and very handsome.

His parents died when he was merely seven years old. He and his brother and sister became orphan in childhood. After the death of his parents their grandmother took them to village Basarke. His grandfather was not a rich man. So in order to make his living he began to sell grams under the shade of a tree on the bank of a tank.

When Guru Amar Dass shifted to Goindwal Bhai Jetha also accompanied them. There Bhai Jetha resumed his work of selling roasted grams. There he found the construction work in full swing. The devotees of Guru Angad Dev had come from far and near and were serving there without taking any wages. Bhai Jetha was very much influenced by the selfless service of the Sikhs. He also made up his mind to become a Sikh of Guru Angad Dev. After selling the grams, he made it his daily routine to help in the construction of buildings. He used also to serve the devotees.

Guru Angad Dev Ji entrusted the Guruship to Guru Amar Dass Ji in 1552 A.D. At that time, the age of Bhai Jetha was about eighteen years.

In December 1552 A.D. one day Mother Mansa Devi said to Guru Amar Dass, "Our daughter Bhaani has now grown up, it is the right time we should select a suitable groom for her." The Guru replied, "It is very proper that you have reminded me that our daughter has reached the marriageable age. But tell me what type of groom should we search for?" Mother Mansa Devi said,

"He should be young, healthy, talented, learned, pious, Gursikh and very handsome." At that time Bhai Jetha had come to meet Guru to take advice for the construction work. When he saw that Mata Mansa Devi had an audience with the Guru, he stood aside. When Mansa Devi saw Bhai Jetha standing near by, then Mother Mansa Devi pointing towards Bhai Jetha said, "The groom should be like this boy." The Guru replied, "He is the only boy who resembles him, there is none else in this world who had the features and qualities like him. If this boy seems you ideal of your imagination as the suitable groom for our daughter Bhaani then why not consider him as suitable groom for her." Mother Mansa Devi had no objection to that.

After few days Bibi Bhaani was married to Bhai Jetha.

Bhai Jetha's service was selfless. Physically he was feeling lowest of lowest but spiritually he always kept his mind in the recitation of the Name of God. Guru Amar Dass was so influenced by his service that he made up his mind to entrust him the leadership of the Sikhs.

One day he asked Sri Ram Dass to take bath. After taking the bath Sri Ram Dass worn new clothes specially tailored for him. The Guru Amar Dass Ji embraced him and guided him to the throne of the Guru and asked him to adorn it. Bhai Jetha (Ram Dass) sat on the throne. Then Guru Amar Dass

placed five paisa and a coconut in front of Guru Ram Dass and after going round him three times he bowed before him. Then Baba Buddha Ji applied the Tilak as a mark of Guruship and spiritual kingdom passed to the fourth Guru.

Guru Amar Dass wanted to colonise a new city. In June 1570 A.D. he took Guru Ram Dass with him and reached the place where he wanted to build a new city.

When Guru Amar Dass and Guru Ram Dass reached at that place, Guru Amar Dass sent for the headmen of the villages of Gumtala, Tung, Sultanwind and Gillwali. The Guru told them that he wanted to colonize a new city at that place. The people of those villages agreed to the proposal of the Guru. Foundation stone of the town was laid by Guru Amar Dass himself and town was named as *Guru Ka Chakk*.

After completion of the Guru Bazar, digging of the Santokh Sar Sarovar started. The workers and masons also constructed houses for their own residences. The Guru also started Langar for the devotees and the workers.

When Guru Ram Dass constructed a Darbar Hall and started preaching

the devotees then the name of the city was changed to Chakk Guru Ram Dass.

The Guru also bought five hundred bighas of land from the nearby village Tung for the further expansion of town.

Rajni, daughter of Duni Chand, a landlord of Patti was married to a leper. She took her husband and reached Guru ka Chakk. She served in the Langar. One day she left her husband by the bank of a small pond in the shade of a 'ber' tree and herself went to Langar.

When the leper was sitting on the bank of pond, he saw a pair of crows dipped down into the pool and flew away with their colour changing from black to white. He considered that the pool did not contain an ordinary water. So he struggled and by crawling reached near the water of the pond. Then he dipped into the water. But when he came out he was astonished to see himself. He was no longer the leper, as he had been a few minutes earlier. He walked as a young man and again sat under the shade of the tree. He waited Rajni very patiently. When Rajni returned from the Langar house, she was distressed to see a new man sitting near her basket. Her husband told

her the complete story of his transformation. But she did not believe it. She took him to Guru Ram Dass who was supervising the construction work inside the city. When the Guru asked the young man to tell the truth, he narrated the whole story which had happened with him. The Guru was convinced to hear the story of the young man as he perceived that pond must be same sacred place about which Guru Amar Dass had told. Then the Guru assured Rajni that young man was her real husband. Her belief in God had cured the leprosy of her husband.

Then the Guru told Baba Buddha Ji that pond was the same holy place about which Guru Amar Dass had foretold. He asked him that there a Pool of Nectar must be constructed.

Next day 'Deg' (a big cooking pot) of Karah Prasad (sweet pudding offered at a Sikh shrine) was prepared. The Guru took Baba Buddha, Bhai Gurdas and other revered Sikhs with him and reached near the Nectar pool. Then the Guru asked Baba Buddha to dig a spade of mud from the tank as an inauguration ceremony of the construction work. After reciting the holy hymns, Baba Buddha Ji dug a spade of mud and threw that in a basket. After that the Karah Prasad was distributed among all the Sikhs.

Then all the Sikhs started digging the mud and filling their baskets were

carrying on their heads and were throwing at the bank. So the digging of the holy tank started from that day.

After completion of the tank four wells were dug at the four corners of the tank. These Persian-wheels were running for twenty four hours and water of these wells was falling in the holy tank.

After the construction of the Amrit Sarovar, the city was renamed as Amritsar.

One day the Guru asked his Sikhs to make arrangements for his departure for Lahore. He took with him all members of his family and some devout Sikhs. When he reached near the Lahore, he saw that all prominent Sikhs and other inhabitants of Lahore had come out to welcome him. They were proud of him that he belonged to Lahore. They perceived that one orphan child due to his selfless service and hard work, had become the True Emperor.

Guru Ram Dass first visited his own house in Chuna Mandi. He stayed there for few days and converted that house into a holy monument.

Making his house a common religious place he stayed in the house of Bhai Sihari Mal. The house of Bhai Sihari Mal was very vast. There devotees were coming to pay homage to the Guru during the whole day. It became very difficult for him to get any time for the recitation of the Name of God. The Guru asked them to observe discipline. He fixed times for assembling. He advised them to come in the morning and evening so that he could fix times for the recitations of hymns and for addressing the congregation. He also started there the common kitchen.

After staying for a long time he returned back to Amritsar along with his family and other Sikhs.

Baba Sri Chand was an elder son of Guru Nanak Dev Ji. When he heard about the construction of the Amritsar city, Nectar Pool and praise of Guru Ram Dass, he came to Amritsar for an audience with the Guru.

At that time he was about ninety years old. Due to worship of God he was still very active and healthy. He was wearing a saffron coloured dress. But he had no affinity with the yogis and recluses. When Guru Ram Dass heard about the arrival of Baba Sri Chand, he rose and himself went to receive Baba

on the way. As he was son of Guru Nanak Dev, so he bowed before him and with great respect took Baba Sri Chand with him and seated him beside him. His few disciples also accompanied him. Baba Sri Chand was very pleased to see the Divine face of the Guru. His face seemed to him resembling the face of his father Guru Nanak Dev. He was fascinated to see the charming personality of the Guru. Then pointing towards the beard of the Guru he said, "Why have you grown such a long beard." The Guru said politely, "It is to wipe the dust of the feet of great men like you." Baba Sri Chand laughed to hear this answer. He said, "It is this humility and politeness which has made you worthy of Guruship. I have heard about your benevolence, generosity and humbleness, but now I have seen with my own eyes. With your devoted service you have not achieved the Guruship but also won the hearts of mankind.

Baba Prithi Chand was elder son of Guru Ram Dass Ji. He was born in 1557 A.D. at Goindwal. He was very zealous, fanatical, cunning and

tactician. Bhai Gurdas has used word (Meena) 'shrewd' for him.

Guru Ram Dass always used to advise him but there was no effect on him. At the time of the construction of Amritsar city and holy tank, he used to embezzle the money offered by the devotees. After few years he became the administrator and was collecting and spending the money himself. He became so conceited that he considered himself as Guru. He had been telling the people that his father was just a nominal head of Amritsar. Actually he had been running the administration. Guru Ram Dass loved his youngest son (Guru) Arjan Dev ardently. So due to jealousy he became an enemy of (Guru) Arjan Dev. He wanted to acquire Guruship by hook or crook. But Guru Ram Dass made up his mind to bestow Guruship to Sri Arjan Dev Ji. At that time Sri Arjan Dev was at Lahore. He sent Baba Budha Ji to bring Sri Arjan Dev back home. Next day he declared him as the next Guru. Baba Budha was asked to apply tilak on his forehead and Guru Arjan Dev became the fifth Guru of the Sikhs.

On Ist September 1581 A.D. Guru Ram Dass went to Goindwal with his family and other Sikhs. He took bath in the Baoli and attended the Darbar. Then he called Guru Arjan Dev to sit near him and said, "Now you are

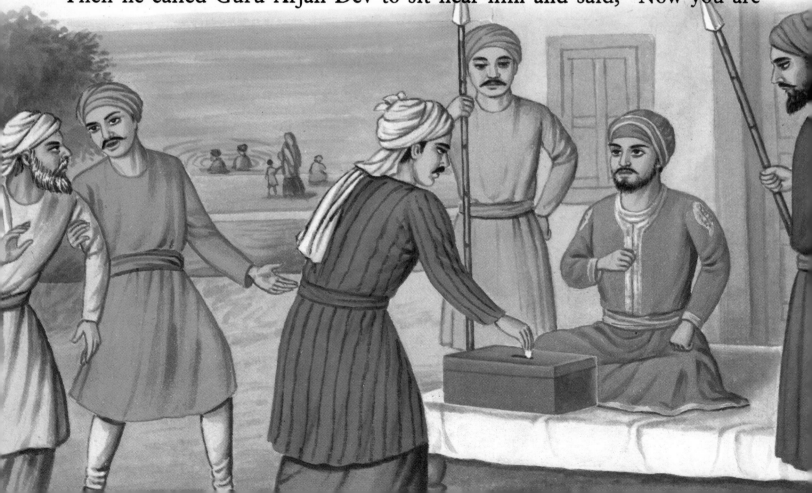

embodiment of four Gurus. The Divine Light travelling from Guru Nanak Dev to Guru Angad Dev from Guru Angad Dev to Guru Amar Dass and from Guru Amar Dass to Guru Ram Dass has now come to you. You are now fifth Guru of the Sikhs. Guru Amar Dass had advised me to construct Amritsar city, a Nectar Tank and Harimandir Sahib. But with in this limited time I have not been able to construct Harimandir Sahib inside the tank. Now I instruct you that you should construct a beautiful Harimandir Sahib inside the Nectar Tank so that the devotees after taking bath in the holy tank, could hear the Divine music sitting inside the Harimandir Sahib.

Then he addressed the congregation and said, "Always recite the Name of God and listen to the hymns sung by the singers. Believe in Guru Arjan Dev who is my embodiment.

Then he closed his eyes and merged into the Supreme Light. All were amazed to see such a miracle.

When Baba Prithi Chand heard about the demise of his father, he atonce rushed towards Goindwal. He forced his maternal uncles to give him the turban of inheritance. But Baba Mohri Ji refused to give him the turban. But Guru Arjan Dev Ji offered him the turban keeping in view the respect of his elder brother.

SRI GURU ARJAN DEV JI

Guru Arjan Dev Ji was born on 15th April, 1563 A.D. at Goindwal. The name of his mother was Bibi Bhaani and Guru Ram Dass, the fourth Guru was his father. Guru Amar Dass was his maternal grandfather, as his mother Bibi Bhaani was the younger daughter of the Guru. At the time of his birth, Guru Amar Dass was enlightening the Sikhs as their spiritual Master. When Guru Amar Dass came to know of the birth of his third maternal grandson, he reached the residence of his son-in-law to see him. Having first glimpse of the child the Guru said, "He will become a great man." Guru Amar Dass was extremely fond of this grandson. Guru Arjan Dev also liked him very much and was always hovering around him. He always used to play in the residence of the Guru. One day Guru Ji advised Bibi Bhaani to bring the child daily without any break. At that time Guru Arjan Dev was four years old. He was very intelligent and he took keen interest in learning Punjabi, holy hymns and music. Within few years he became well-versed in these subjects. Guru Arjan Dev had a sweet voice. He used to sing the hymns according to the specified Raags (Measures).

When Guru Arjan Dev was eleven years old Guru Amar Dass made up his mind to get married his youngest grandson. As the Guru loved him very much he wanted to see him married during his life time.

Guru Amar Dass betrothed him to daughter of Krishan Chand of village Mau in Doaba. On the fixed day the marriage party rode towards the village Mau. After crossing the river Beas the marriage party reached village Mau. All the residents of the village came out to receive the marriage party.

Then the headman of the village met Guru Amar Dass and said, "It is my request that there is a tradition of this village that before entering the village the bridegroom has to lance out a peg dug in the field.

All the members of marriage party were equipped with swords, lancers and spears. On Guru's direction, one young man handed over one lancer to Guru Arjan Dev. He was already riding on a horse. Holding the lancer in his right hand, he drove the horse towards the peg and drew out the peg at the very first attempt. The people of the village were astonished to see such an extraordinary feat of   Guru Arjan Dev.

Once obliging the orders of his father, Guru Arjan Dev reached Lahore and attended the marriage. After the conclusion of the marriage he shifted to Chuna Mandi, the childhood residence of his father. Guru Ram Dass had converted that house into a Gurdwara. During his stay there Guru Arjan Dev was reciting music daily. He had a sweet voice and was competent to play all types of musical instruments. When the Sikhs heard that a son of Guru Ram Dass was himself reciting sacred hymns, and himself was providing music to it they thronged to hear the hymns of the Gurus from the sweet voice of Guru Arjan Dev. In the morning and evening a Diwan was held and the strength of the devotees was increasing day-by-day. In those days Sain Mian Mir was considered one of the sacred and respected saints of India. People of all religions were going to pay homage to Sain Mian Mir. Guru Arjan Dev reached the residence of Sain Mian Mir to meet him. Sain Mian Mir had a great respect for Guru Nanak and his followers. He was very pleased to see him. He asked him to sit near him. He was very impressed after hearing the views of Guru Arjan Dev about Sikh philosophy.

Though he himself was Peer of Peers, he became a great devotee of Guru Arjan Dev.

Bhai Manjh was a devout Sikh of Guru Arjan Dev Ji. He always engrossed himself in the service of the Guru. He daily went to the forests to bring dry sticks for the free kitchen. He always kept himself busy in the service of the Guru. One day when he was returning to Amritsar, carrying a bundle of sticks on his head, a dust storm of very high speed blockaded him. There became a pitch darkness all around. But reciting the Name of the God he carried his movement forward. On his way there was an old well. As he could not see it, he fell into the well. But he kept the bundle of sticks on his head so that it might not get wet.

In the evening when Sikhs found that Bhai Manjh had not reached there. They at once ran towards all sides for his search. When one party reached near a well they heard recitation of the holy hymns. When they peeped into the well they found that Bhai Manjh was standing in the well, keeping dry sticks on his head. They ran towards Darbar Sahib and brought ropes in order to bring Bhai Manjh out of the well. They downed the rope into the well and asked him to catch the rope so that he might be pulled out. But Bhai Manjh said, "First bring out the dry sticks so it could be used for the kitchen." So he tied the rope to sticks and the Sikhs brought out the sticks then he himself caught the rope and came out of the well. Seeing his great

devotion Guru Arjan Dev blessed him eternal enlightenment.

To implement the order of his father Guru Arjan Dev planned to construct Harimandir Sahib at the same platform. He thought to build such a temple that should be unique in the world. This temple should be only used for contemplation, devotional singing, recitation of hymns and for meditation on the Name of God. The Guru himself planned the basic fundamentals of the construction work. He thought that temple should have four doors, so that it might be open to all. These doors must not be in any known direction such as East, West, South or North, as Hindus worship in the direction of East and Muslim worship in the direction of West. So he planned that each door should be in the middle of two directions. He also thought that temple should be kept low than the surface of the earth, so that whoever enters the temple premises first lowers himself which would be a sign of humility. He also selected Sain Mian Mir to lay the foundation stone. That was a secular thinking of the Guru. Sain Mian Mir had great regard for Guru Arjan Dev. When the Guru stayed at Lahore for two years he used to meet Sain Mian Mir on alternate days.

The Guru invited Mian Mir to lay the foundation stone of the new temple. Mian Mir showed no hesitation and came to Amritsar with his followers. He was respected by the people of all religions. He was a great learned man.

He laid down the foundation stone of Harimandir Sahib on October 3, 1588 A.D. He placed four bricks in the centres of four directions and one placed in the middle of the four. Then Guru Ji asked Sikhs to distribute 'Karah Prasad' to the congregation.

After the construction of the Darbar Sahib daily Darbar was held there and devotional singers sang the holy hymns.

The Guru laid the foundation stone of Kartarpur in December 1594 A.D. It is said that instead of fixing a branch of a tree as the foundation stone, a tree itself was entombed. That is called as 'Thamm' and at Kartarpur a very beautiful Gurdwara 'Thamm Sahib' has been built at that spot. After construction of some residential buildings, the Guru dug a big well named as Gangsar. The Guru told the people of that area that water of Gangsar was

more pious than the water of Ganga. So instead of going to Ganga they should take bath in the water of Gangsar.

When the Guru found that his wife was keen to have a child, he asked her to go to Baba Buddha for his blessing. Baba Buddha was respected by the Sikhs and the Guru alike. Mata Ganga with her attendants reached Guru Ki Beedh. When Baba Buddha saw the wife of the Guru carrying the food on her head and coming on foot, he rose up and welcoming her said, "I was feeling very hungry today, it seems my mother has brought food for me." He was delighted to eat the simple food. While crushing the onion with his fist he said, "Your son will crush the head of the enemies the way I have crushed the onion. He will be very brave and strong."

Guru Arjan Dev thought to remain away from his jealous brother Prithi Chand. He shifted to village Wadali four miles away from Amritsar.

According to the blessing of Baba Buddha Ji (Guru) Hargobind was born on June 9, 1595 A.D. at village Wadali. The Sikhs rejoiced at the birth of Hargobind, but Prithi Chand and his wife lost the balance of their mind. For them only way to get the Guruship was to kill the new born child. So they planned to kill the child one way or the other. There was one old nurse in the house of Guru Arjan Dev. Prithi Chand paid her some money and took

her into confidence. She smeared her nipples with poison. She took the child with great love, but when she tried to rise up in order to go to safe place, she fainted and fell down. The poison applied to her nipples had affected her. When she found that she was at the verge of death, she confessed her guilt and told the family that Prithi Chand had bribed her to kill the new born child.

After some time he sent a snake charmer. He demonstrated his show in two or three houses and then entered the house of the Guru. Family members and other Sikhs residing there came out to see his show. The child Hargobind was also enjoying the show with great interest. When the snake charmer found that child was taking great interest he sent one snake towards the child. Child Hargobind caught the snake from the head and rubbed it on the floor with such a force that snake died at the spot. All were astonished to see this brave act of the child. The Sikhs interrogated the snake charmer and he confessed that Prithi Chand had sent him to kill the child.

Baba Prithi Chand settled at village 'He-ar' near Lahore. There he

constructed his own Harimandir and declared himself the real fifth Guru. But he tried again and again to eliminate Guru Arjan Dev. He met officers of Mughal regime and bribed them to invade Amritsar. He met Sulhi Khan and offered a large sum of money. Sulhi Khan agreed to invade Amritsar. Sulhi Khan was a revenue officer of the Mughal court. He said, "I will get permission from the Subedar of Lahore that I have to raid Amritsar to collect the tax dues."

According to commitment Sulhi Khan reached 'He-ar' with his squad. Prithi Chand served them various delicacies. Prithi Chand took Sulhi Khan with him in order to show him his new type of bricks-kilns. When they reached near the kiln, Sulhi Khan's horse startled at the sudden flight of a bird. The horse was so frightened that it jumped over the wall and fell into the burning kiln along with Sulhi Khan. Sulhi Khan was burnt completely and was reduced to ashes. This plan of Prithi Chand also failed, and the army troops returned back.

Meharban compiled a granth in which he included hymns of four Gurus and poetry of Peers-Faqirs. He mixed hymns of

Sikh Gurus and his own in such a way that it became a difficult task to sort out the true and false hymns.

When Guru Arjan Dev heard about it he decided to take immediate steps to stop the confusion. He called a meeting of Bhai Gurdas, Baba Buddha Ji and other prominent Sikhs. In the meeting they adjudged that hymns of Sikh Gurus and Bhagats (Saints) should be compiled in one volume. Guru Arjan Dev deputed Baba Buddha as incharge of Darbar Sahib. In order to complete this arduous task he himself camped at the bank of Ramsar tank. He took the services of Bhai Gurdas to write the hymns.

The holy Granth was compiled in three years. This monumental work was completed in 1604 A.D. (Bhadon Sudi Ekam Samvat 1661 Bikrami).

Jahangir was against Guru Arjan Dev since a long time even when he had not become the King of India. When he was going to Kashmir, he summoned Guru Arjan Dev to meet him at Lahore. He asked the Guru to revise the holy Granth and to add in it some hymns in praise of Mohammad. The Guru did not agree. Then he asked the Guru to embrace Islam. But the Guru said, "It is better to die than to change religion."

As he did not bow before the demands of Jahangir, the Qazi gave an injunction ordering the Guru to be tortured to death. He was tortured for five days. But the tyrants found that he was bearing all the torments with perfect peace. On the fifth day Guru asked for a bath in the river Raavi. He was allowed. The Guru was saying again and again, "Sweet is your Will, O God! The gift of Your Name only I seek." Reaching the river, he walked into the water and disappeared. He never came out of the water.

SRI GURU HARGOBIND SAHIB JI

Guru Hargobind Sahib was born on June 9, 1595 A.D. at village Wadali. This village is at a distance of four miles from Amritsar. Now this village is known as Guru-Ki-Wadali. Seeing such a handsome personality of the young Guru Hargobind many rich men were approaching Guru Arjan Dev for the engagements of their daughters to Guru Hargobind.

Chandu Shah was a minister of the King at Delhi. He sent his emissaries to Punjab in order to find a suitable groom for her daughter. Hearing the grandeur of the Darbar of Guru Arjan Dev, they reached Amritsar. When they attended the Darbar, they found Guru Hargobind (age ten years) also sitting beside the Guru. They were captivated to see the sharp features of Guru Hargobind. They at once made up their mind to engage the daughter of Chandu Shah to Guru Hargobind. They informed the Guru about their proposal. But the Guru said, "I am a Faqir and it is not possible for me to have relation with such a richman.

At the time of adoration of Gurgaddi, when Baba Buddha offered him the sacred headgear, he refused respectfully and wore a turban with a very precious plume prepared specially for the occasion. Then he asked Baba Buddha to bring a sword. Baba Buddha brought one sword and in confusion put it on the wrong side. When the Guru noticed it, he asked him to bring an other sword. He said, "I will gird two swords, one sword of Shakti (power) and other sword of Bhakti (meditation). So in this way Guru Hargobind combined in him Peeri (Renunciation) and Meeri (Royalty). From that day the Guru advised his Sikhs to get themselves armed and to offer him only the weapons and horses. He said, "Those Sikhs who will join our army would be trained in the modern type of warfare, they would be given clothes twice a year and free meals in the kitchen."

When the Sikhs came to know about this, thousands of them joined the Guru's Army. They enjoyed the celestial music in the morning and evening and got training of arms in the day time.

When Murtaja Khan, Nawab of Lahore, noticed that Guru had constructed a fort at Amritsar and was also strengthening his army, he informed about it to King Jahangir. When Jahangir came to know about this he at once sent Wazir Khan and Guncha Beg to Amritsar in order to bring Guru Hargobind Sahib. Guru Hargobind was detained in fort of Gawalior. In the fort the Guru met many princes who were detained there due to political reasons. They were leading a very deplorable life.

In the meantime Sain Mian Mir met Jahangir and got the Guru released. The fifty-two princes who had been detained due to political reasons or for committing default, were pining in fort for years. The Guru left the fort with all fifty-two princes. As the Guru liberated the fifty-two princes so he is known as Bandichhod (Liberator). Jahangir became a great admirer of the Guru.

One day King Jahangir invited Guru Hargobind to accompany him for a hunting expedition. The Guru who himself was a great lover of this game, accepted the invitation. During the expedition when they entered the dense forests, a tiger attacked the King. The Royal party who was accompanying the King, shot many bullets at the tiger, but due to panic they could not harm the tiger. It appeared as if the tiger was about to kill the King. When Guru Hargobind saw it, he dismounted from his horse and pulled out his sword and stood against the tiger. He carried his shield in his left hand. When the tiger saw that another man was standing before him, he jumped with great force and attacked the Guru. But the Guru struck his shield on the head of the tiger with such an aggression that tiger fell on the ground. Then with a speed of lightning the Guru pierced his sword in the belly of the tiger. When the King found that tiger was lying dead, he came near the Guru and admired his bravery. He said, "I have not seen such a gallant hero. You have killed the lion single handed as if it was a cat or a dog." Then the King

became a great friend of the Guru and always invited the Guru, for the hunting expeditions.

First battle was fought at Pipli Sahib. The army of the common people faced the royal army. Then the Guru ordered his army to enter the fort of Lohgarh. The gate was closed. When Mukhlis Khan found that the Sikhs had hidden themselves in the fort he beseized the fort.

But as the sun had set, so they were forced to camp outside. When the Sikhs found that Mughal army was resting outside without any fear, they took the stone gun and threw shower of stones on the enemy.

Next day Painde Khan took the command of the Sikh army and opened the gate. He challenged Didar Ali a close associate of Mukhlis Khan but he could not even bear his first blow. He was killed there and then.

Then Guru fell upon Mukhlis Khan and in the twinkling of an eye he killed him with one blow. When Mughal army saw that Mukhlis Khan had been killed, they ran away. The Guru asked his Sikhs not to chase the running army.

Once Bhagwan Dass father of Rattan Chand was killed by the Sikhs. Rattan Chand met Abdulla Khan, the Subedar of Jalandhar and complained against the Guru. Abdulla Khan was already against the Guru. So he commanded an army of four thousand soldiers and attacked Sri Hargobindpur. When the Guru was informed about this he alerted his Sikhs. When the Mughal army reached near the city, the Sikhs welcomed them with bullets and arrows. Abdulla Khan did not know that the Sikhs were so well equipped. All Sikhs were in their trenches so it was impossible for the Mughals to trace them. The Mughal army became reinless and they ran away towards the safe places. Abdulla Khan tried very much to put them under his control, but he failed.

When Shah Jahan heard about the defeat of Abdulla Khan he ordered his army to ruin the city of Sri Hargobindpur. But Wazir Khan told him, "The Guru was constructing a mosque for the Muslim inhabitants of the city, but Bhagwan Dass was against it." When Shah Jahan heard this, he ordered to confiscate the property of Abdulla Khan.

Once Guru Hargobind Sahib reached village Bath. The village Bath was abode of Baba Sri Chand. There he met Baba Sri Chand and showed great respect for him. Baba Sri Chand was also very pleased to see the Guru and his sons. The Guru along with his sons sat near him. He narrated to him the episodes of the Sikh battles. But Baba Sri Chand was looking towards Baba Gurditta with great curiosity. His features resembled Guru Nanak. Then Baba Sri Chand said, "How many sons are in your house." When the Guru told him that he had five sons. Baba Sri Chand said, "From these five whom you consider to offer to Baba?" The Guru said, "My all five sons belong to you. You can choose any one for your service." Then Baba Sri Chand pointing towards Baba Gurditta said, "If this son is your Tikka (elder son) then he is also my Tikka (elder son). Now he has become elder son of this world and the next world." Then he got up and offered his "Seli Topi" the reverend turban of Udaasis to Sri Gurditta Ji and said, "The throne of Meeri Peeri of Guru Nanak has already been transferred to your house. Now I also bestow the throne of Darveshi to your house."

When Bhai Gurdas perceived that his hour of death was near, he sent a message to Guru Hargobind Sahib. When the Guru received the information he at once rushed to Goindwal. When Bhai Gurdas found the Guru near him, he felt very happy. The Guru asked the Sikhs to recite the holy hymns and himself sat near Bhai Gurdas. He pressed the head and hands of Bhai Gurdas and blessed him. Bhai Gurdas saw towards the Guru and said, "I am now going to leave this world. Please advise the Sikhs that when I breathe last, they should recite the Name of God. After performing my last rites no memorial or tomb should be constructed. My residual bones and ashes should be immersed into the river Beas." After a few days Bhai Gurdas breathed his last. The dead body of Bhai Gurdas was carried by Guru Hargobind Sahib, Baba Bhana, Bhai Jetha and Bhai Bidhi Chand. Thousands of people attended the funeral procession. Guru Hargobind Sahib himself lit the pyre. After performing the last rites, he asked his Sikhs to recite hymns from the holy Granth.

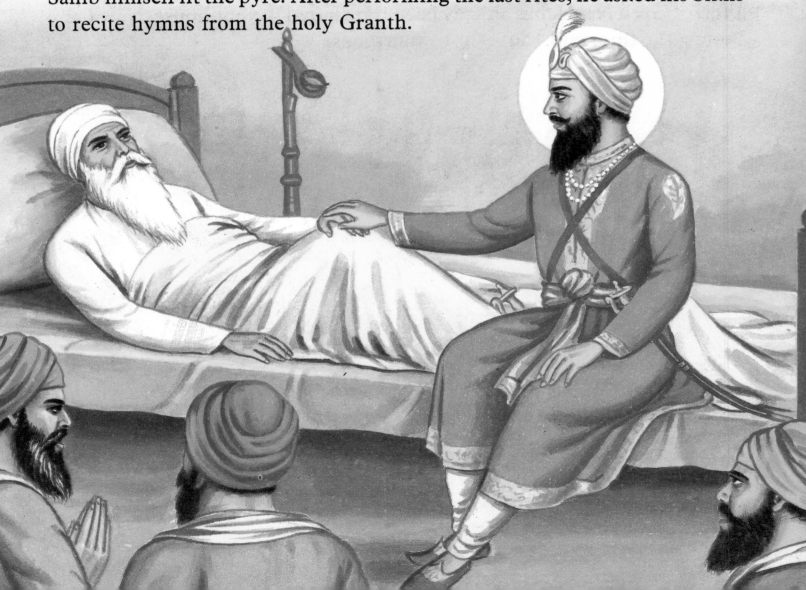

At Kiratpur one day Guru Hargobind Sahib and his elder son Baba Gurditta Ji went to see Baba Budhan Shah. After paying homage to the elderman, the Guru said, "Father! Please give us that milk which Guru Nanak had promised to take as the sixth Nanak." Baba Budhan Shah at once became alert and saw them with great curiosity. He said, "Light of God is same but countenance and embodiment is different. If you show me the same divine face of Guru Nanak then I would be very pleased to offer you the milk." The Guru asked Baba Gurditta to go to home to take bath. When he returned his face exactly resembled the face of Guru Nanak. Sain Budhan Shah was surprised to see the real embodiment of Guru Nanak. Sain Budhan Shah bowed before him in great reverence and requested him to sit. Then he brought two bowls of milk and offered to the Guru and Baba Gurditta.

Sain Budhan Shah's all doubts and suspicions vanished. Whatever he asked Baba Gurditta, he found the true answer. At last the desire of Baba Budhan Shah was fulfilled. His soul was delivered from the body and he was exempted from further transmigration.

One day Baba Gurditta went to Jungle to play the game of hunting. His one friend mistook cow as a deer and killed it. When the owner of the cow found it, he began to weep. When they offered him the price of the cow he refused to take money. Instead he said, "I want my cow alive, you are the son of Guru you can return back my cow." He again began to weep loudly. Baba Gurditta took pity on him and by reading the Gurmantar he revived the cow.

The story of making the dead cow alive reached the ears of Guru Hargobind Sahib. When he heard this he became very angry and he called for Baba Gurditta and reprimanded him for his such misdeed. He said, "When have you become partner of God? Life and death are in the hands of God. Who are you to give life to the dead?"

Baba Gurditta was loving the Guru so much that he could not bear his displeasure and resentment. He went near the tomb of Baba Budhan Shah and sat in meditation. While contemplating the Name of God he merged his human light with the Supreme light. When Guru Hargobind Sahib heard about it, he became very grieved.

SRI GURU HAR RAAE JI

Sri Guru Har Raae was born on Magh Sudi 13 Samvat 1687 (30 January, 1630 A.D.) at Kiratpur. Baba Gurditta, the eldest son of Guru Hargobind Sahib was his father. Baba Gurditta had two sons and name of the elder son was Dhir Mal. At the time of his birth, Guru Hargobind Sahib was at Amritsar. When he heard the news of the birth of his grandson, he was so pleased that he said, "Customer of a great object has come."

Guru Hargobind reached Kiratpur after a few days. On his way he distributed alms to the poor. Reaching Kiratpur first he visited the room of the child. He was pleased to see the celestial face of the child. He took the child in his lap and blessed him with many boons. He said, "This child has come to make this world more pleasant. He will play a great role in uniting the people with the Name of God.

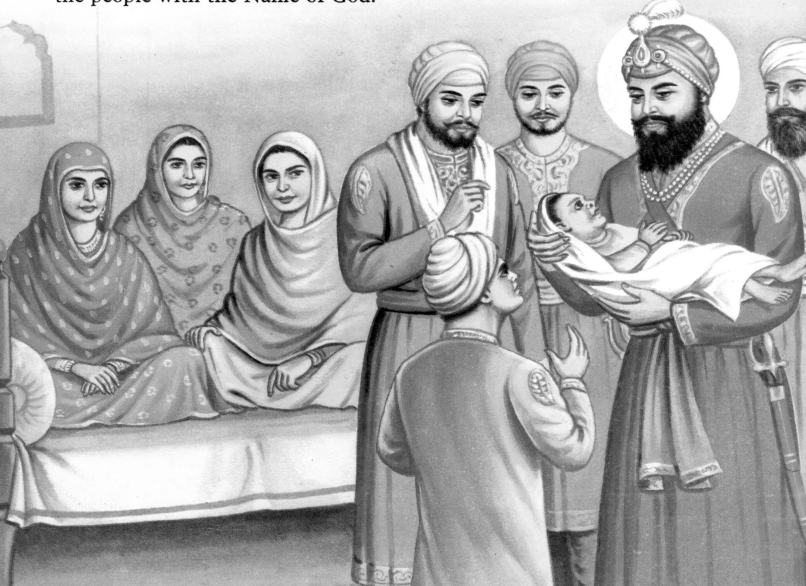

Guru Hargobind Sahib was always keeping (Guru) Har Raae with him. Wherever he went, he took (Guru) Har Raae with him. In the company of his grandfather he acquired the good qualities of Guru Hargobind Sahib. When the Guru found that Dhir Mal was a very cunning and clever fellow he concluded that he was not suitable for the Guruship. So he made up his mind to bestow Guruship on Guru Har Raae.

The Guru called for Guru Har Raae and asked him to sit on his throne. The devotees saw the face of the Guru Har Raae with great curiosity. They were amazed to see celestial face of the Guru Har Raae. Then Guru Hargobind Sahib placed five coins and a coconut in front of Guru Har Raae and bowed before him. After the grandson of Baba Buddha Ji, Baba Bhana offered him a sword and tied aigrette to his turban. After applying a 'Tilak' on his forehead,   he bowed before him.

King Aurangzeb was a very cruel man. Whoever helped Dara Shakoh, King Aurangzeb got him killed. As the Guru Har Raae had also helped Dara, so Aurangzeb wanted to kill the Guru. So he sent his generals thrice to annihilate Kiratpur. Firstly he sent Zalam Khan with ten thousand armed forces to invade Kiratpur. But while on his way he took the uncooked meat of an animal and died due to severe pain in his stomach. Aurangzeb again sent his another general Dhoode Khan of Kandhar to attack Kiratpur. When he reached Kartarpur his one enemy killed him while he was asleep. When soldiers saw their commander dead, they returned back.

Third time Aurangzeb entrusted this task to general Nahar Khan who was ruler of Saharanpur. But when the army of Nahar Khan reached Yamana Nagar, cholera spread in the army. The soldiers were dying like sheeps and goats. Nahar Khan died with half of his army

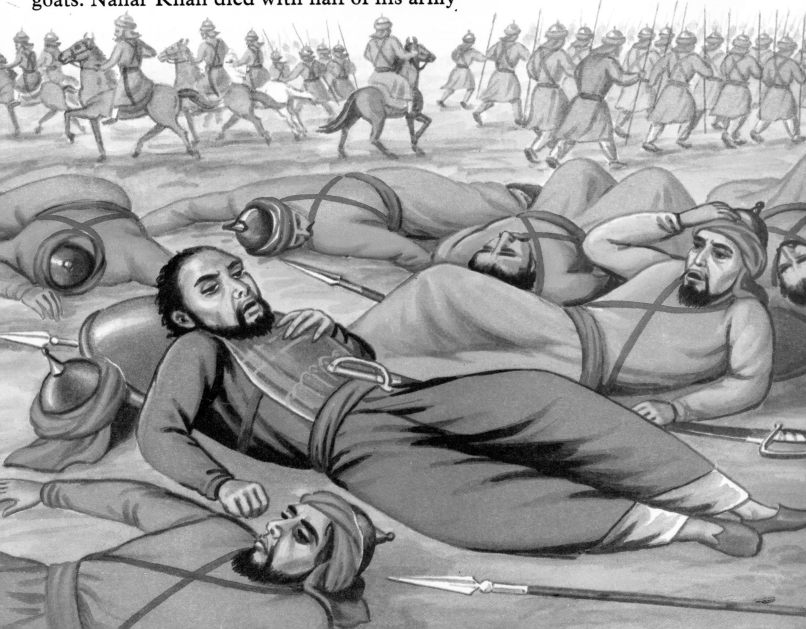

SRI GURU HARKRISHAN JI

(Guru) Harkrishan, the eighth Guru of the Sikhs was born on 7th July, 1656 A.D. at Kiratpur. His Father was Guru Har Raae Ji and the name of his mother was Mata Krishan Kaur Ji. At the time of his birth Guru Har Raae Ji predicted that the child would do such a great deed, which had not been done so far in the world.

One day (Guru) Harkrishan saw a wounded snake. A large cluster of ants were scratching his flesh. The snake was in great trouble. He tried very hard to run away, but ants swarmed around in such a way that he could not move even an inch. On seeing such a critical condition of the snake, (Guru) Harkrishan said, "What is the guilt of this snake that such a large number of ants has been eating his flesh and he has been fluttering with pain." Hearing this Guru Har Raae said, "This snake was a deceitful monk in his previous birth. He was befooling the simple and religious minded people. These ants are those simple people whom he looted with cunning contrivances. (Guru) Harkrishan was amazed to hear such a story of an old rich monk.

Guru Har Raae Ji installed Guru Harkrishan Ji as the eighth Guru. He ignored his elder son Baba Ram Raae. But when Baba Ram Raae heard about this, he complained to Aurangzeb.

Aurangzeb atonce asked Raja Jai Singh to send a call to Guru Harkrishan to see him in Delhi. Raja sent his Diwan Paras Ram with some horsemen to bring the Guru with him. He reached Kiratpur after two days. He handed over Guru one letter from Raja Jai Singh and one letter from king Aurangzeb. Next day those letter were read in the Darbar. The Guru sought the advice of Baba Gurditta Ji, Bhai Dargah Mal Ji and Bhai Mani Singh Ji. They asked the Guru to go to Delhi. But he told them he would not meet the king. He would not go against the wishes of his father. He said, "I am not afraid of the king, I will keep the promise at any cost."

When Raja Jai Singh was informed about the arrival of the Guru, he came to receive the Guru accompanied by his officers and Sikh devotees.

The Guru asked his devotees to go to their villages. They all returned

back. **Raja Jai Singh took** the **Guru,** his mother **Krishan Kaur** and other honourable disciples **to his** banglow. They stayed in one separate portion of that Banglow. **After two** days Raja Jai Singh met the Guru and said, "My Lord ! **King Aurangzeb** wants to meet you. Where would you be like to adjoin?"

The Guru said boldly, "At the time of departure I had already told your minister **Paras Ram** that I would not meet king Aurangzeb at any cost. Neither I will attend the Darbar nor I allow to see him at your Banglow. Your minister had assured me that you would not ask me to meet Aurangzeb." Raja Jai Singh and his courtiers were astounded by hearing such bold reply from the young Guru. They were amazed to see such a determination of the Guru. They did not try to persuade him. Raja Jai Singh had a great respect of the Guru, but he was forced by Aurangzeb to ask the Guru.

Aurangzeb sent for Raja Jai Singh. He told him that he wanted to test the insight of the young Guru. Aurangzeb said, "You should dress your wife as

a maid-servant and one of your maid-servant should be dressed as a queen. If the Guru recognises your wife then I will be convinced that he possesses spiritual powers." Raja Jai Singh agreed to arrange the drama. Rani dressed herself as a maid servant. One of the maid servant was dressed with very precious clothes and jewels. When Raja Jai Singh was satisfied he went to meet the Guru. On meeting he said, "My Lord ! My queen is very anxious to see you. Please come in our palace so my queen and other servants could have a glimpse of you. They all are waiting for you."

The Guru agreed to accompany him. When he entered the palace, the maid servant dressed as queen came to welcome the Guru. But the Guru did not take notice of her. He straight went in front of the real queen. Standing before her he said, "What was the eventuality for a queen to do such a type of hypocrisy. We are Faquirs and such humbugs does not appear good for a queen of Raja Jai Singh.

Aurangzeb wanted to see Guru Harkrishan Ji, but he declined. He was ready to face any dire consequences. During those days small pox epidemic was at rage in Delhi. The disease was increasing day by day. The Guru made up his mind to cure the patients. They were getting a relief by mere a glimpse of him. He determined to take the disease of all patients on himself. At last he himself became a patient of smallpox.

Though he fell seriously ill, but he still attended the patients. The devotees were wondering that the rage of the smallpox was steadily declining but the health of Guru was deteriorating gradually. When the worried congregation asked him to explain them the enigma of such developments then the Guru smiled and said, "O Beloved of the Guru! I have come here to cure the residents of Delhi from the horrible disease of smallpox; this disease can leave the patients on one condition. If some holy man dare to take the disease on himself then they can be saved from the rage of the disease. I have determined to take the disease of all the patients on myself." When the devotees asked about the next Guru, Guru Harkrishan said, "Baba at Bakale" which indicated that he was pointing towards Guru Tegh Bahadur Ji

SRI GURU TEGH BAHADUR JI

(Guru) Tegh Bahadur was born in Baisakh Vadi five 1678 Bikrami (1st April, 1621 A.D.) at Amritsar. His mother was Mata Nanaki the second wife of Guru Hargobind Sahib. He was the youngest son of Guru Hargobind Sahib. At the time of his birth Guru Hargobind Sahib was hearing the singing of the holy hymns of 'Aasa di Vaar' at Darbar Sahib. He was informed about the birth of fifth prince at the completion of the singing of the hymns. He at once came to his house. Historians write that when the Guru saw the new born child he bowed in reverence and said, "When this child will be grown up he would shield the poor and down-trodden. He will save the bleeding and helpless humanity. He would be a prophet of love, truth and peace. I have bowed before the sun of reality. He would uproot the cruel Kingdom of Mughals."

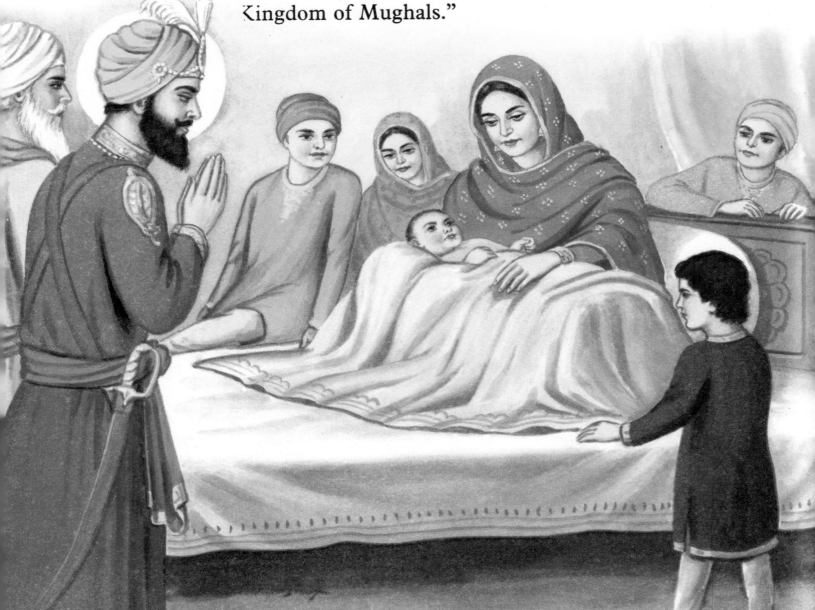

(Guru) **Tegh Bahadur** and **Baba Attal Raae** used to play with their playmates. One day when they were playing, due to sun set darkness prevailed. At that time the turn of seeking came on the head of a boy named Mohan. When next day Baba Attal **Raae Ji** and (Guru) Tegh Bahadur went to play, they found that Mohan was **not** present among their playmates. They all thought that Mohan had not **come** due to his turn to seek. They at once determined to go to the house of Mohan. When they reached there they found that Mohan was lying dead on his bed. His parents were weeping. They told them that a poisonous snake had bitten Mohan and he had died. But Baba Attal Raae did not believe them. He said, "He is just pretending because to-day is his turn to seek. In order to avoid his turn he has been sleeping and you are weeping as if he had **died. I am** going to strike him with my stick and he will get up." When Baba **Attal Raae Ji** hit him with his stick, then to the astonishment of all, **Mohan got up and** became alive.

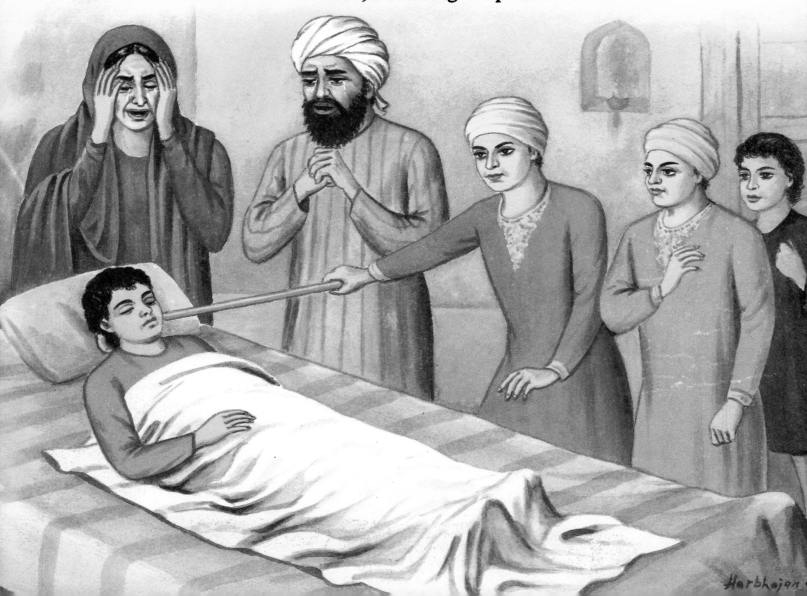

By the times of the birth of (Guru) Tegh Bahadur, Sikh schools of education had significantly advanced. Baba Buddha Ji and Bhai Gurdas Ji were great scholars of Punjabi. When (Guru) Tegh Bahadur was four years old he was sent to Ramdas where Baba Buddha Ji was teaching Punjabi to the Sikhs. There he taught Punjabi and Sikh discipline to his disciples. He was not only teaching Punjabi but also was conferring on them lessons of honest and high living. Though he was very old, but still he was working in the fields. (Guru) Tegh Bahadur was very influenced by the life of Baba Buddha Ji. It was result of his education that when (Guru) Tegh Bahadur was staying at Bakala, he was not taking offerings from his admirers but instead he worked in the fields and earned his livelihood with his own hands. He lived there a very humble life and never realized the people that he was son of Sodhi Sultan Guru Hargobind Sahib. From Baba Buddha Ji he also got the strength of stout determination. After completing his education from Baba Buddha Ji, he was entrusted to Bhai Gurdas for higher education. Bhai Gurdas was a scholar of great talent.

When the family of Guru Hargobind was staying at Kartarpur, a devout disciple of Guru Hargobind Ji, Bhai Lal Chand one day met the Guru and requested him to engage his daughter Gujri with (Guru) Tegh Bahadur. He was thirteen years old at that time. The Guru accepted his offer and marriage was fixed for February, 1634 A.D. The Guru invited all his relatives. (Guru) Tegh Bahadur and Guru Hargobind were dressed in colourful uniforms. There robes were jewelled and embroidered with golden threads. Sri Tegh Bahadur looked like a prince. When the marriage party reached the house of Bhai Lal Chand, he along with his relatives came to receive the marriage party. He also received a beautiful garland from the Guru. There was a great hustle and bustle on that day. The people of the surrounding areas came to see the fire works.

The marriage party was served with rich meals. At the time of departure of the marriage party, Lal Chand bowed before Guru and said, "I am not capable to give anything in dowry." The Guru embraced him and said, "When you have given your daughter you have given us everything."

When Guru Harkrishan Ji at the time of his departure to the heavenly

abode could not name his successor and uttered only two words 'Baba Bakale' then interested parties interpreted it according to their own perceptions. 'Baba Bakala' meant that Guru was at Bakala. So about 22 pretenders posed themselves as the true Gurus and established their Manjis there. Makhan Shah reached Bakala to give his offering to the Guru. But he was confused to find so many Gurus. So Makhan Shah decided to offer two gold mohras to each self-styled Guru. Makhan Shah tested all the pretenders but no one asked him about the five hundred mohras. Bhai Makhan Shah knew that Sri Guru Tegh Bahadur younger son of Guru Hargobind was staying permanently at Bakala. First of all Makhan Shah met mother Nanaki. He expressed his desire to meet the Guru. Mother Nanaki guided him to the underground apartment where Guru Ji used to sit for meditating on the Name of God. Makhan Shah was amazed that their prevailed a celestial bliss on the face of the Guru and atmosphere was calm and peaceful. He atonce placed five hundred gold mohras in front of the Guru and bowed in reverence. The Guru blessed him. Makhan Shah joy knew no bounds. He atonce rushed to the roof of the house and waving his girdle shouted, "I have found the true Guru, I have found the true Guru."

According to historians the Guru reached Amritsar on 22nd November, 1664 A.D. along with his disciples. First they took bath in the holy tank and then they decided to pay homage to holy temple. But when they reached doors of the holy shrine, they found its entrance doors closed. In the evening a Sikh belonging to nearby village Walla requested the Guru to shift to their village. The Guru agreed and they all rode towards village Walla.

When the women of Amritsar came to know about the coming and departure of the Guru due to unfavourable attitude of the masands, they at once assembled and reached Walla. There they found that the Guru was staying in the house of Mata Haro. They at once met the Guru and placing the gifts which they had brought with them, infront of the Guru, bowed and requested, "Our True Lord ! Forgive us, it is not the fault of the people of Amritsar. It is all due to the priests of Harimandir who had not allowed you to enter in the holy shrine. Amritsar is the city of your birth place. You are Lord of that city and we are your faithful followers. We have come to take you back to Amritsar. Please allow us to serve you for few days, "The Guru was pleased to see such strong affection of the women of Amritsar. He blessed them, "Maaiaan Rab Rajaaee-aan" (Ever blessed be the women of Amritsar).

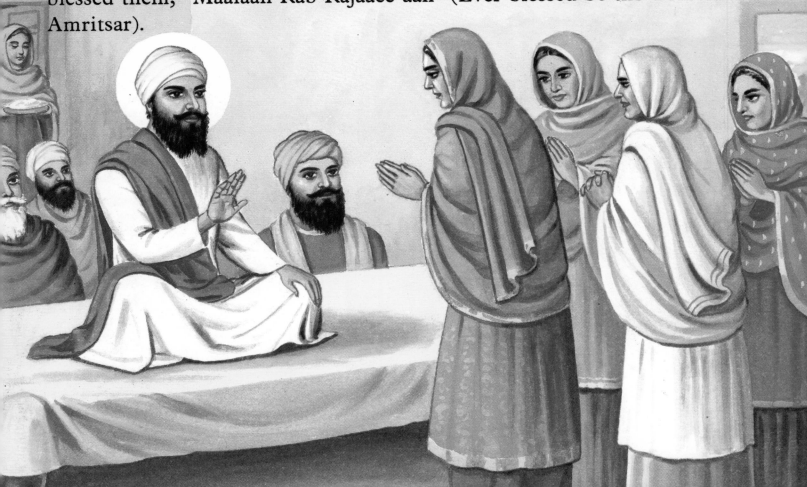

Guru Ji bought the land of Makhowal and built the city of Anandpur. Construction work was still carrying on when Guru Ji made up his mind to travel the country in order to preach the teachings of Sikhism. He started his journey towards the region of Malwa.

Peer Bhikhan Shah was a great devout of Guru Nanak Dev. Under his guidance Saif Khan also became a devotee of Guru Nanak Dev. When he was informed that Ninth Nanak had been travelling in the region of Malwa then he sent messengers to request the Guru to pay a visit to his house. The Guru accepted his invitation and reached the Garden of Nawab Saif Khan. Nawab Saif Khan received the Guru with great pleasure. He also presented very costly gifts to the Guru. Nawab Saif Khan furnished very beautiful rooms for the residence of the Guru. Nawab was a very religious man so he always discussed with Guru on spiritual topics. In Sikh and Muslim religions there are many common beliefs. Like Muslims Sikh believe on one God. They do not worship idols. To attain the salvation they stress on prayer.

At the time of departure the Nawab presented beautiful chariot and horses.

Travelling through the country, Guru Ji reached Dhaka. There he stayed

in the house of one masand named Bulaaki Dass. One day his mother requested the Guru that she wanted to keep a portrait of Guru Tegh Bahadur with her. The Guru advised her that there was no need to keep a portrait, whenever you would recite the Name of God, you would get everything. But she requested him again and again. Then Bulaaki Dass called for an expert artist to draw the portrait of the Guru. A famous Muslim artist of Dhaka started to prepare the portrait. With in a day, he drew all other parts of the Guru's body, but when he started to draw the face of the Guru with his brush, his brush stopped moving. He could not confront the glow of the face of the Guru. So he showed his inability to trace the face of the Guru. Then the Guru took the brush from the artist and drew his face himself. (It is said that picture is still kept in the Museum of Kolkata). Then the Guru handed over that portrait to that old lady. She was very pleased to have the portrait of the Guru.

When Raja Chakardhawaj of Assam heard that a large Mughal army had been marching towards Assam in order to attack him, he made elaborate military preparations to meet the army. He also pressed into service many magicians and witchcrafts, who were expert in their arts in order to scare the enemy. There also lived a great magician woman named as Dhoban Witch.

At night Dhoban witchcraft with the power of her magic flooded the water of river Brahamputra and the Mughals camping in the low areas were washed away with their belongings. But when she found that the Guru and the army of Ram Singh remained uneffected, she hurled a twenty six feet long stone, the four sides of whose girt measured 36 inches x 28 inches x 28 inches x 33 inches. The stone came flying across the river like a missile and struck ground near Guru Tegh Bahadur. It struck the ground so hard that nearly half of it penetrated into the ground and about thirteen feet remained standing out of the ground at an angle of about fifty degrees. Even today this stone is standing there in the same position.

When Dhoban witchcraft found that the large stone had done no damage to the Guru and his associates, then she pulled a big tree along with its roots and hurled it towards Guru. The tree also fell near Guru Tegh Bahadur and was dug into the ground along with its roots and remained alive and green. That tree of (Pipal) is still standing there.

When the Raja Chakardhawaj saw that Dhoban witchcraft had done no damage to the Guru and the army then he sent

Dhoban witchcraft to meet the Guru. Dhoban came and fell at the feet of the Guru. She requested the Guru that two Rajas should reconcile with each other. The Guru accepted her request and settled the affairs amicably.

Preaching all the way, the Guru Tegh Bahadur reached Anandpur Sahib in 1671 A.D. When the Guru was satisfied that the construction of residential buildings, Diwan Halls and rest houses had been done according to his plannings then he sent a messenger to Patna giving him a letter to send for his family. Staying at many places in the way, they reached Lakhnaur near Ambala. There they stayed in the house of Jetha masand. They were forced to stay there for a month due to rainy season. Then they proceeded towards Anandpur Sahib.

The Guru received his family with great love. The Child Guru also paid a homage to Guru Tegh Bahadur with great reverence. The Guru also asked the Child Guru to sit near him as the devotees were very anxious to have a glimpse of the Divine Child. On that day a large number of people had come to attend the holy congregation. All eyes were centered on him. They were feeling blessed by having a glimpse of the beloved Child.

Aurangzeb understood that Brahmans of Kashmir were considered very

sacred. So if they embraced Islam then the other Hindus of the lower classes would not mind to come into the fold of Islam. So he issued orders to the Governor of Kashmir to force Brahmans to embrace Islam. The Governor of Kashmir atonce took strict actions.

They were informed by someone that there was only one man, Guru Tegh Bahadur who could save their religion. Under the leadership of Pandit Kirpa Ram, they met Guru Tegh Bahadur. They told him their story of sufferings. On hearing their dreadful and terrible story, the Guru was very much moved. He looked sad and thoughtful.

At that time Child Guru Gobind Raae entered inside and stood by the side of his father. The Child Guru saw that the persons who were standing before his father were feeling very sad. They were figures of gloom and agony. Guru Tegh Bahadur was also sitting in a very pensive mood. Seeing all this the Child Guru said, "My dear Father ! Why are you feeling so sad and thoughtful." Guru Tegh Bahadur related him the story of the woe of the Pandits. He said, "My son the cruel rulers have become shameless, they are forcing Hindus to embrace Islam. Those who refuse, are put to death. This tragedy can be averted only if one noble soul lays down his life to fight against   this injustice." Hearing this

Gobind Raae said, "Who else can be more worthy than you ?"

The Guru atonce made up his mind and said, "Go and send this message to Aurangzeb that if he can bring their spiritual leader Guru Tegh Bahadur into the fold of Islam, then all Brahmans are ready to embrace Islam."

Aurangzeb summoned Guru Ji at Delhi and asked him to embrace Islam. But the Guru was very rigid in his stand. At last, the royal Qazi issued orders that the Guru should be beheaded.

In order to frighten Guru, Bhai Mati Dass was sawn, Bhai Dayala was thrown into cauldron of boiling water and Bhai Sati Dass was burnt alive by wrapping cotton around his body. But the martyrdom of these brave disciples did not effect the Guru. He remained calm and peaceful.

The King ordered that Guru Tegh Bahadur should be beheaded in the public place and an announcement should be made about this dreadful incident.

Executioner Jalal-ul-Din severed the head of the Guru with one blow. It is said that after execution a blind sand storm encircled the area.

SRI GURU GOBIND SINGH JI

(Guru) Gobind Singh was born at Patna on 22nd December, 1666 A.D. His father was Guru Tegh Bahadur Ji and the name of his mother was Mata Gujri Ji. Guru Gobind Singh assumed Guruship on 11 November, 1675 A.D. at Anandpur Sahib. Baba Ram Kanwar, a descendant of Baba Buddha Ji performed the ceremony of Guruship. He presented the Guru, a garland of pearls, plumed turban, one sword, one horse, one falcon and five coins of gold. Guru Ji looked very handsome and smart while sitting at the throne of Guruship. The congregation was full of joy and happiness. The musicians were reciting the holy hymns.

After assuming the Guruship, Guru Gobind Singh presented Siropas to Baba Ram Kanwar, Baba Gurditta Ji and other devotees.

In Kabul there lived a very rich man, whose name was Duni Chand. He was a great devotee of the Guru.

They prepared such a magnificent tent that it surpassed the beauty of the

king's tent. This woollen tent was so big that even Guru Ji held his great Darbars in that tent.

That tent was presented to Guru on the occasion of Baisakhi in 1680 A.D. The devotees from Kabul, Kandhar, Balkh, Bukhara and Gazni brought many other presents. Most important articles in those gifts were, rugs, carpets, woollen blankets and bed covers.

When hill-chiefs saw that tent, they were very much amazed and strayed. They felt small, as the Guru was owner of such a tent, which even surpassed the beauty of king Aurangzeb's tent.

The ruler of Assam state Raja Rattan Raae alongwith his mother and other ministers reached Anandpur Sahib on the occasion of Diwali. The royal family were honoured to stay in the Kabuli tent. Then the presents were offered to the Guru.

The Guru was greatly pleased to see the presents. Raja first presented a singular weapon, five in one, out of which five types of weapons could be made-pistol, sword, lance, dagger and club. Second gift was a wonderful throne from which stepped out puppets to play chess. Third gift was a

drinking cup of a precious metal. As a fourth gift five beautiful horses with splendid trappings were offered to the Guru. But of all these presents the most wonderful present was a black elephant. This elephant was unique in appearance and was trained to perform various acts of service. He had a white stripe stretching from the tip of trunk along the forehead and back, right upto the end of his tail. This elephant waved "Chaur" over the Guru, for washing the feet of the Guru, he held a jug of water in his trunk and after washing Guru's feet, he wiped them with a towel.

Guru Ji had made up his mind to fight the tyrants with sword. So, he was enlisting the new recruits in his army everyday. Guru Ji realized that without a drum (Nagaara) military equipment was incomplete. He called Diwan Nand Chand and ordered him for the construction of a big Nagaara.

But in those days only kings could beat a drum in their own kingdom. No king would allow another king to march through his area with the beat of drum.

But Guru's mother Mata Nanaki Ji advised him to devote himself to religious affairs only. After hearing mother's advice calmly, Guru said, "My dear mother, my religion and religion of my forefathers inspires me to take up arms. I tell you what I am doing, I am doing according to the Will of God. Almighty had sent me in this world to uproot the tyrants and uplift the down trodden. Now I will not sit in seclusion. Now I must accomplish the mission of Guru Nanak. According to wish of God, tyrants have to be disarmed and evils doers have to be destroyed. I am not afraid of hill-chiefs. I bear them no malice and I have done them no harm." At last a great Nagaara was prepared and Guru Ji named it 'Ranjit' or the victorious on the battle-field.

The first marriage of the Guru took place on 23rd of Haar, Samvat 1734, with Mother Jito Ji, the daughter of Sri Harjas Raae resident of Lahore. This marriage was arranged at 'Guru Ka Lahore' near Anandpur Sahib.

The Guru's second marriage was solemnized with Mata Sundri, daughter of Ram Sharan resident of Lahore, in 1684 A.D. The Guru's third marriage was performed with Mata Sahib Deva daughter of Bhai Ramu Bassi Khatri

of Rohtas in 1697 A.D. at Anandpur. The Guru had four sons and the name of the eldest son was Baba Ajit Singh. He was born to Mata Sundri Ji on 22nd Baisakh, Samvat 1743 Bk. (26th Jan.1687 A.D.) at Paunta Sahib. It is said that when Guru Gobind Singh Ji had won the battle of Bhangaani and the Sikhs were enjoying the celebrations, the Sahibzada was born. As they had won the battle so he was named 'AJIT' (unconquerable). Baba Ajit Singh while fighting for great cause died a saint-soldier's death on December 22, 1704 A.D. at Chamkaur Sahib.

Baba Jujhar Singh the second son of the Guru, was born to Mata Jeeto Ji on 14 Asuj, Samvat 1747 (1690 A.D). He was also very brave and dauntless warrior. When the Guru left Anandpur Sahib for good, he also accompanied him to Chamkaur Sahib.

During the battle of Chamkaur Sahib, when he saw that his elder brother had died fighting bravely against the Mughals, he also requested the Guru to allow him to go in the battle-field. There he fought so bravely that Mughals were astonished at the deed of valour of a young boy of fourteen years. Killing a band of tyrants Baba Jujhar Singh died on December 22, 1704 A.D.

Baba Zorawar Singh the third son of Guru Gobind Singh Ji was born to Mata Jeeto Ji on 12 Saawan, Samvat 1753 Bk. (17th Nov. 1696 A.D.).

He was slain by Nawab of Sirhind on Poh 13,1761 Bk. (December 27, 1704 A.D.). The place where their bodies were cremated, a Gurdwara called Joti Sarup stands. The place where the two Sahibzadas were bricked and beheaded stands the Gurdwara, called Fatehgarh Sahib.

Baba Fateh Singh younger son of Guru Gobind Singh was born to Mata Jeeto Ji on Phagan Sudi 7, Samvat 1755 Bk. (25th Feb. 1699 A.D.). He was also bricked alive and then beheaded with his elder brother Baba Zorawar Singh on December 27, 1704 A.D. by Nawab of Sirhind. The city of Fatehgarh Sahib is named after his name. This city has now become a headquarter of a district.

On the day of Baisakhi of 1699 A.D. a big and a beautiful tent was set up at the place of Keshgarh Sahib. Behind the throne of the Guru, a small but beautiful tent was also erected.

When the Guru entered inside the tent, all people were amazed to see him. His eyes were shining like fire, his face was glowing with a celestial bliss, his naked sword was glittering in his uplifted right hand and his whole body

was looking like that of a great warrior, who had just rushed into the battle field.

He said with a thundering voice, "This goddess, Bhagauti is always hungry for the heads, today she wants the heads of my dear Sikhs."

A Sikh rose up and said, "O true Lord! My head is always at your service. The name of that Sikh was Bhai Daya Ram, a resident of Lahore.

The Guru caught him by his arm and took him into that small tent which was set up behind his throne. Then the people heard a severe blow of the sword and a stream of blood rushed out of the tent.

Similarly, Bhai Dharam Singh, Bhai Mohkam Singh, Bhai Sahib Singh and Bhai Himmat Singh were dragged into the tent and they met the same fate. At the end when the Guru came out of the tent he was not alone, there were five others, who were looking like him. They were those 'five one's' who had offered their heads to the Guru. All men were astonished to see five men alive and wearing beautiful robes. Then a drink called Amrit was prepared and was administered to Panj Pyaras. Then the Guru asked the Panj Pyaras to administer baptism to him. After that the Guru invited all the Sikhs to receive baptism. Word *Singh* was added to the names of men and *Kaur* to the names of women. The Guru asked them to take an oath to keep five K's namely *Kes* (hair), *Kangha* (comb), *Kirpan* (daggar), *Karra* (bracelet) and *Kachha* (short drawer).

Those five Sikhs who had offered their heads to the Guru at his amazing

call were honoured by the Guru naming them as his five 'Beloved Ones'.

Bhai Daya Singh belonged to Lahore, an important city of Punjab. He was born in Samvat 1726 Bk. The Name of his father was Sri Sudha Khatri and his mother's name was Srimati Diaali. He stayed with Guru at Talwandi Sabo and helped him in compiling his literary and religious works. He accompanied the Guru while going to Nanded, Deccan, and always served him with great devotion. He died at Nanded in Samvat 1756 Bk.

Bhai Dharam Singh belonged to Hastinapur (Delhi). He was born there in Samvat 1723 Bk. The name of his father was Sri Sant Ram, who was Jat by caste. His mother's name was Srimati Sabho. He died at Nanded in 1765 Bk.

Bhai Mohkam Singh was born in Dwarka (Gujrat) in Samvat 1720 Bk. The name of his father was Sri Tirath Ram who was a washerman by caste. He died at Chamkaur Sahib on Dec. 2, 1704 A.D.

Bhai Sahib Singh was a resident of Bidar (Karnataka). He was born in Samvat 1719 Bk. His father Sri Chamna was a poor barber of Bidar. His mother's name was Srimati Sonabai. He died while fighting at Chamkaur Sahib on December 22, 1704 A.D.

Bhai Himmat Raae was born at Jagannath (Orissa) in Samvat 1718 Bk. His father Sri Gulab Raae was a water carrier (Jheewar) by caste. The name

of his mother was Srimati Dhanno Devi. Guru Nanak Dev Ji had visited Jagannath during his Udaasis.

Once a *Jatha* of Majha Sikhs was going to Anandpur Sahib. This Jatha also included a young baptized woman. Her name was Bibi Deep Kaur. When the Jatha reached the village Talabban, they saw a well. They halted near well in order to drink water. But as Bibi Deep Kaur was not feeling thirsty, she continued to march on. When she had gone some yards away from his companions, four armed Mohammadans saw her. Finding her alone, they decided to loot her. They rushed towards her and ordered her to stop. When she stopped, they commanded her to hand over all her belongings to them. But Bibi Deep Kaur was not an ordinary Indian woman, she displayed the gallant Sikh spirit. As she was also armed, she was not afraid of them. With a healthy presence of mind, she threw one of her gold bangle on the ground. When one of the dacoits bent down to pick up the bangle, she took her sword and severed away his head with in no time. When the other three saw that horrible scene, they were completely bewildered. But before they could decide, she killed the other two with her powerful sword. When the fourth tried to run away, she pursued and killed him.

When the hill-chiefs were certain that they could not defeat the Guru in

the field. So they made up their mind to invade the city. They blocked the city for two months, but they achieved nothing. So they decided to break the gate of fort in order to occupy it. They intoxicated an elephant, covered his body and head with iron-plates and directed him against the gate of the fort.

When the Guru got this information he asked his one trusted and brave soldier Bhai Bachittar Singh to face the elephant.

Bachittar Singh came out of the fort with his gallant horse taking his great lancer in his right hand and gave such a powerful blow to the face of the elephant that it pierced through the steel armour. The severely wounded elephant turned round and ran about killing his own army men. Bachittar Singh pursued the elephant crying loudly. Then the Khalsa army also fell on the hill-chiefs. The hill army took to their heels and ran away in all directions to save their lives.

The Guru was very much pleased to see the bravery of Bhai Bachittar Singh. He patted him lovingly and gave him a beautiful sword as a symbol of honour.

The lancer with which Bhai Bachittar Singh wounded the intoxicated elephant, is kept in the fort of Keshgarh at Anandpur Sahib.

Bhai Ghanhaiya belonged to village Sodra in district of the Gujjranwala (Pakistan). He was Guru's devout Sikh and had a very delicate and kind heart. His peace loving nature desisted him from becoming a soldier. But being a beloved Sikh of the Guru, he wanted to serve him one way or the other. So he learnt the art of rendering first aid to the wounded. He organized an ambulance band who were serving the wounded in the battle-field. When

and wherever fighting took place he would take his men with him. He served the water and provided other necessary help to the wounded. He dressed their wounds and also helped them to reach their camps. He was serving the friends and enemies alike.

One day few Sikhs complained to the Guru that Bhai Ghanhaiya was giving first aid and water to the wounded enemies and Sikhs alike. They also accused him that practically he was helping the enemy, as the soldiers, who had been cured by him, were again becoming fit to face the Sikhs. The Guru called Bhai Ghanhaiya and asked him about the accusations ascribed by other Sikhs. Bhai Ghanhaiya said, "My Lord ! It is true, I provide water and first aid to all wounded persons though they might be Turks or Sikhs. But actually I am neither serving Sikhs nor Turks, I have been serving you. Your teachings have opened my mind and I see you in every human body which lies wounded on the battle field. So I am supplying water and providing first aid to none else, but you." The Guru was very much pleased to hear this answer and he stood up and patting him said, "Bhai Ghanhaiya, you are great, you have achieved your target, you have crossed the worldly ocean and now have been exempted from

further transmigration. In those days red cross societies did not exit, so Bhai Ghanhaiya is claimed to be the pioneer of red cross.

When the generals of the royal army found their soldiers being killed in large numbers, they lost the hope of defeating the Sikhs in the open field. Therefore they made up their minds to besiege and blockade the fort and to cut off all supplies. But when the long siege did not bear any fruit the royal army and hill-chiefs were also worried. Then they requested the Guru to evacuate Anandpur Sahib. They also swore on the cow and the Quran.

But the Guru knew the treacherous plans of the hill-men and the Turks.

He told the envoys of hill-men and Turks that he would evacuate the fort if the armies first allow the removal of his precious property. They at once agreed and assured the Guru of their promises made. Then the Guru asked his men to fill the sacks with old shoes, torn clothes and other rubbish material. The sacks which were covered with beautiful brocade, were loaded on the backs of bullocks which were forced out of the fort at mid night. Flambeau with long handles were tied to the horns of the bullocks, so that those might be seen from a long distance. When the animals reached near the army, they at once fell upon them to loot the (so called) precious property.

But when they touched the foul smelling rubbish, they felt ashamed.

After few days the Guru vacated the fort and reached Chamkaur. At Chamkaur the Guru entrenched the mud-built house. His army consisted of only forty trusted Sikhs, his weapons of offence and defence were those which he and his Sikhs had arranged to bring with them. The Guru asked his eight Sikhs to guard each wall, two were posted at the gate and two were directed to keep watch. The Guru himself, with his few Sikhs and two sons, held the top storey.

At mid night the Mughal army rushed up and surrounded the village. Next morning a part of army advanced to capture the small fort. But when they approached near the fort a valley of bullet and arrows greeted them.

Then next party advanced, they also met the same fate.

At last the Mughal army decided to break through the gate of the fort. But as they tried to rush forth in that direction the Guru despatched a Jatha of five Sikhs to face them. They fought very bravely and killed a large number of Mughal soldiers. Then the Guru sent an other batch and they also faced the attackers valiantly. Then Baba Ajit Singh requested the Guru for permission to go out and to face the enemy. The Guru permitted him to go out side. Five Sikhs accompanied him. They all fought very bravely. They sacrificed their lives for the true cause. In the next batch Baba Jujhar Singh fought as bravely as his brother had done. He also died fighting to the last. It was night by now. The Mughal army lay down to take rest. Then the Guru had ten Sikhs left with him. They took counsel together and requested Guru

118

to leave the fort. The Guru obeyed their command and left the fort with three other Sikhs– Bhai Daya Singh, Bhai Dharam Singh and Bhai Maan Singh.

At Machhiwara the Guru and his three Sikhs stayed in the house of Bhai Gulaba. He was very anxious to serve them but was also afraid of the Muslim rulers. One day and one night Gulaba kept them on the upper storey of his house. There also lived two Rohilla Pathans– Ghani Khan and Nabi Khan. They were horse traders and they had sold many horses to the Guru. When they heard about the Guru, they were moved to tears and they decided to help the Guru. They dyed khaddar blue and prepared robes and dresses as worn by a sect of Muslim saints. Guru and his three Sikhs dressed themselves in these clothes and let their long hair fall down their shoulders.

Disguising themselves in that way, the Guru sat on a litter and it was lifted by Ghani Khan, Nabi Khan, Maan Singh and Dharam Singh. Bhai Daya Singh waved a 'chaur' over him. In that way they were escorting the *Uch da Peer*. On the way nobody questioned them and they travelled on safely. Reaching Raikot the Guru stayed with Raae Kalha who was a rich and influential Muslim Jat of Raae Kot. He served the Guru with loving hospitality.

From Raae Kalha, the Guru went to Dina Kangar. At Dina Kangar, the Guru enrolled many brave soldiers and also collected ammunition and

weapons of war. Here he came to know that Nawab of Sirhind was pursuing him. He therefore decided to go into thick jungles where defence would be easier.

The Guru had already sent messengers to all areas where his trusted gallant warriors had been living. When the people of Majha received this news, they resolved to go to the Guru and to die fighting for him. A Jatha of two thousand armed Singhs under the command of Mai Bhaago of Jhabal and Bhai Mahaan Singh of Sursingh started towards the pond of Khidraana.

Under the guidance of Wazir Khan, a large Mohammadan army reached there. Mai Bhaago, Bhai Mahaan Singh and their associates came out from the shrubs and fell on the royal army. Mughal army was astonished to see such an on slaught. It was very hot on that day. It became very difficult for the Mughal forces to face the Sikhs. So they ran back. Sikh army chased them. Nawab of Sirhind was very humiliated by this defeat. He did not dare again to attack the Guru. When Guru Gobind Singh found that Majha Sikhs had defeated the Mughal forces, he felt very happy. About forty Sikhs were lying dead. The Guru blessed the martyrs as the Muktas (saved one's). In their memory now at that place stands a city named as Mukatsar (The tank of saved one's).

From Khidraana, the Guru advanced towards Talwandi Sabo. He renamed city as Damdama Sahib. There he dictated from his memory the whole of the Guru Granth Sahib and gave it a final form, which is considered to be the most authentic. Bhai Mani Singh wrote the Granth in his own hand writing. The Guru re-edited the Granth Sahib in order to add in it the holy hymns of Guru Tegh Bahadur at proper places.

After staying for about nine months at Damdama Sahib the Guru decided to go towards South. Though his disciples requested him to give up the idea of going towards South but the Guru had to accomplish the task assigned to him by God.

Meanwhile Bhai Daya Singh and Bhai Dharam Singh who had gone to deliver the letter of victory to Aurangzeb, returned back and met the Guru. They informed the Guru about Aurangzeb's last request that he wanted to meet him. The Guru decided to accept the Aurangzeb's last wish and made up his mind to go to Ahmad Nagar but when he reached near Baghpur, he heard the news of the death of Aurangzeb.

From Baghpur Guru Ji proceeded towards south and reached Nanded. There he met a yogi named Madho Dass.

The Guru baptized him and renamed him Banda Singh Bahadur. Then he was told about the miserable condition of the Punjab.

The Guru allowed him to go to Punjab and advised him to punish the enemies of the Sikhs. The Guru gave him a Nagaara (Drum) and a banner as emblems of authority and handed him five arrows from his own quire as a pledge of victory. The Guru also asked five Sikhs, Baba Binod Singh, Baba Kahan Singh, Baba Baaz Singh, Baba Rann Singh and Baba Daya Singh to accompany him and to help him; he also gave him Hukamnamas addressed to important Sikhs of the Punjab, instructing them to help Banda Singh in any way.

At the time of departure, the Guru also ordained him to remain pure in conduct and never to see or touch an other's wife; to be true in word and deed and to consider himself as the servant of the Khalsa.

Baba Banda Singh gladly accepted the orders of the Guru and after touching Guru's feet he set out for Punjab along with his companions.

One day a Pathan stabbed the Guru, when he was resting inside his tent. The Sikhs were struck with grief and anxiety. The Guru consoled them and told them that there was nothing to worry. Immediately the wound was washed and sewed. When the emperor came to know about this incident, he sent two English doctors, who resewed the wound and applied proper medicine.

The Guru became hale and hearty very soon. As usual he began to attend the Darbar. One day he asked Bhai Daya Singh to bring five coins and a coconut. At that time musicians were singing the holy hymns. The Guru got up and leaving his throne went before the Granth Sahib. This Granth he had compiled at Damdama Sahib. He bowed before the Granth Sahib and placed five coins and a coconut in front of it. Then he got up and addressing the congregation said,

As ordained by the Lord, a new way of life is evolved.
All the Sikhs are asked to accept the Holy Granth as the Guru.
Guru Granth should be accepted as the living Guru.
Those who wish to meet God, will find Him in the holy Word.

ANSWER SHEET

1. What were the names of the father and mother of Guru Nanak Dev?

2. What was the name of the mid wife attending at the time of birth of Guru Nanak Dev?

3. While making horoscope, what Pandit Hardyal predicted about Guru Nanak Dev?

4. Who was ruler of Talwandi at that time?

5. What was the name of the physician, who had come to diagnose the illness of Guru Nanak?

6. Who was Nawab of Sultanpur, when the Guru was working there as a Modi?

7. What was the name of the eldest son of Guru Nanak Dev?

8. Who accompanied Guru Nanak during his travels?

9. Who invaded India during life time of Guru Nanak?

10. To whom Guru Nanak nominated his successor?

11. What is the name of the town where Guru Angad Dev preached Sikhism?

12. Write about the main works performed by Guru Angad Dev during his Guruship?

13. To whom Guru Angad Dev named his successor?

14. What was the name of the wife of Guru Angad Dev?

15. Which Mughal Emperor met Guru Angad Dev at Khadur?

16. Which Mughal Emperor met Guru Amar Dass?

17. What is the name of the city where Guru Amar Dass preached Sikhism.

18. Who established Amritsar city?

19. To which Guru, Baba Sri Chand son of Guru Nanak himself met?

20. Which Guru compiled and edited Sri Granth Sahib.

21. By the order of which Mughal Emperor Guru Arjan Dev was martyred at Lahore?

22. Who succeeded Guru Arjan Dev as Sixth Guru?

23. Who laid the foundation stone of Harimandir Sahib?

24. Who was seventh Guru of the Sikhs?

25. Where did eighth Guru die? Of which disease did he die?

26. Who declared that he had found Guru Tegh Bahadur as the real Guru?

27. For what cause Guru Tegh Bahadur laid down his life.

28. Name the Sikhs, who were martyred along with Guru Tegh Bahadur?

29. Where Guru Gobind Singh was born?

30. What is the name of the city, which was constructed by Guru Tegh Bahadur?

31. Describe how Guru Gobind Singh created Khalsa?

32. Name the five beloved one's?

33. Name the five kakkaar's, which are essential part of a real Sikh?

34. Name the four princes of Guru Gobind Singh?

35. What was the name of Guru Gobind Singh's mother?

36. Who succeeded Guru Gobind Singh as the next Sikh Guru?

37. Name the ten Gurus?

38. From Nanded Guru Gobind Singh sent some Singhs to organize Sikhs in Punjab. Who was leader of those Singhs?

39. Why Guru Gobind Singh compiled and edited Sri Guru Granth Sahib again at Damdama Sahib?

40. Who helped Guru Gobind Singh while compiling Sri Guru Granth Sahib?